WATCHING WILDLIFE
GALÁPAGOS ISLANDS

David Andrew

Lonely Planet Publications
Melbourne Oakland London

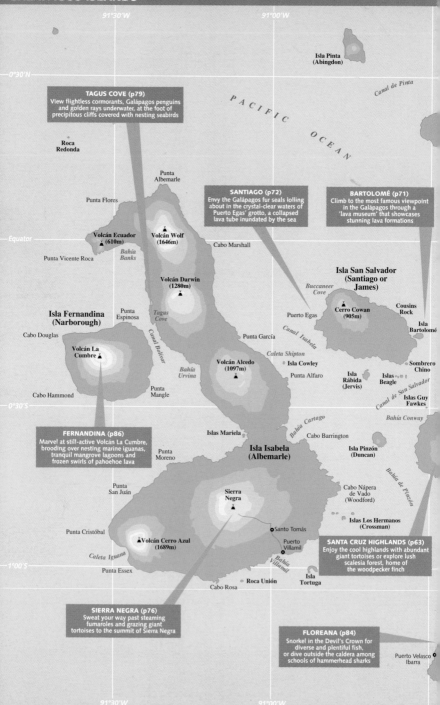

GALÁPAGOS ISLANDS

TAGUS COVE (p79)
View flightless cormorants, Galápagos penguins and golden rays underwater, at the foot of precipitous cliffs covered with nesting seabirds

SANTIAGO (p72)
Envy the Galápagos fur seals lolling about in the crystal-clear waters of Puerto Egas' grotto, a collapsed lava tube inundated by the sea

BARTOLOMÉ (p71)
Climb to the most famous viewpoint in the Galápagos through a 'lava museum' that showcases stunning lava formations

FERNANDINA (p86)
Marvel at still-active Volcán La Cumbre, brooding over nesting marine iguanas, tranquil mangrove lagoons and frozen swirls of pahoehoe lava

SIERRA NEGRA (p76)
Sweat your way past steaming fumaroles and grazing giant tortoises to the summit of Sierra Negra

SANTA CRUZ HIGHLANDS (p63)
Enjoy the cool highlands with abundant giant tortoises or explore lush scalesia forest, home of the woodpecker finch

FLOREANA (p84)
Snorkel in the Devil's Crown for diverse and plentiful fish, or dive outside the caldera among schools of hammerhead sharks

PACIFIC OCEAN

Isla Pinta (Abingdon)

Canal de Pinta

Roca Redonda

Punta Albemarle

Punta Flores

Volcán Ecuador (610m)

Volcán Wolf (1646m)

Cabo Marshall

Equator

Punta Vicente Roca

Bahía Banks

Volcán Darwin (1280m)

Isla San Salvador (Santiago or James)

Buccaneer Cove

Cerro Cowan (905m)

Cousins Rock

Isla Fernandina (Narborough)

Punta Espinosa

Tagus Cove

Puerto Egas

Isla Bartolomé

Cabo Douglas

Canal Bolívar

Punta García

Canal Isabela

Sombrero Chino

Volcán La Cumbre

Caleta Shipton

Cabo Hammond

Bahía Urvina

Volcán Alcedo (1097m)

Isla Cowley

Punta Alfaro

Isla Rábida (Jervis)

Islas Beagle

Islas Guy Fawkes

Canal de San Salvador

Punta Mangle

Islas Mariela

Bahía Cartago

Bahía Conway

Cabo Barrington

Isla Isabela (Albemarle)

Isla Pinzón (Duncan)

Bahía de Pinzón

Punta Moreno

Punta San Juán

Sierra Negra

Cabo Nápera de Vado (Woodford)

Islas Los Hermanos (Crossman)

Volcán Cerro Azul (1689m)

Santo Tomás

Punta Cristóbal

Caleta Iguana

Puerto Villamil

Bahía Villamil

Punta Essex

Cabo Rosa

Roca Unión

Isla Tortuga

Puerto Velasco Ibarra

91°30'W

91°00'W

0°30'N

0°30'S

1°00'S

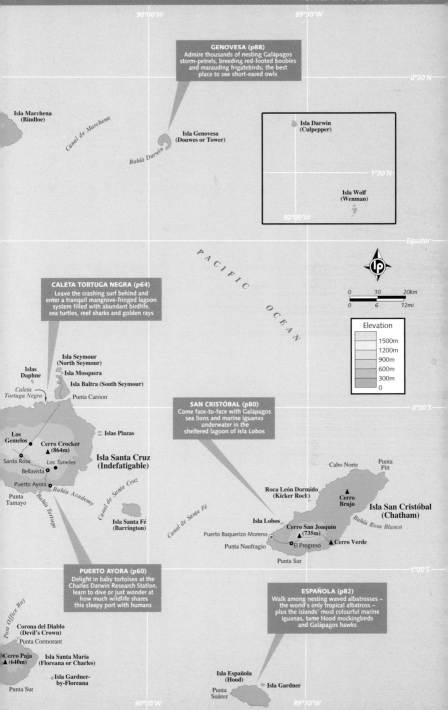

GENOVESA (p88)
Admire thousands of nesting Galápagos storm-petrels, breeding red-footed boobies and marauding frigatebirds; the best place to see short-eared owls

CALETA TORTUGA NEGRA (p64)
Leave the crashing surf behind and enter a tranquil mangrove-fringed lagoon system filled with abundant birdlife, sea turtles, reef sharks and golden rays

SAN CRISTÓBAL (p80)
Come face-to-face with Galápagos sea lions and marine iguanas underwater in the sheltered lagoon of Isla Lobos

PUERTO AYORA (p60)
Delight in baby tortoises at the Charles Darwin Research Station, learn to dive or just wonder at how much wildlife shares this sleepy port with humans

ESPAÑOLA (p82)
Walk among nesting waved albatrosses – the world's only tropical albatross – plus the islands' most colourful marine iguanas, tame Hood mockingbirds and Galápagos hawks

PACIFIC OCEAN

Equator

Elevation
1500m
1200m
900m
600m
300m
0

0   10   20km
0   6   12mi

Isla Marchena (Bindloe)

Canal de Marchena

Isla Genovesa (Douwes or Tower)

Bahía Darwin

Isla Darwin (Culpepper)

Isla Wolf (Wenman)

Isla Seymour (North Seymour)
Isla Mosquera
Isla Baltra (South Seymour)
Punta Carrion

Islas Daphne

Caleta Tortuga Negra

Los Gemelos
Cerro Crocker ▲ (864m)
Santa Rosa
Los Tuneles
Bellavista
Puerto Ayora
Punta Tamayo

Isla Santa Cruz (Indefatigable)

Islas Plazas

Bahía Academy

Canal de Santa Cruz

Isla Santa Fé (Barrington)

Canal de Santa Fé

Bahía Tortuga

Cabo Norte
Punta Pitt

Roca León Dormido (Kicker Rock)

Cerro Brujo ▲

Isla San Cristóbal (Chatham)

Bahía Rosa Blanca

Isla Lobos
Puerto Baquerizo Moreno
Cerro San Joaquín ▲ (735m)
El Progreso
Punta Naufragio
Cerro Verde ▲
Punta Sur

Post Office Bay

Corona del Diablo (Devil's Crown)
Punta Cormorant

Cerro Paja ▲ (640m)
Isla Santa María (Floreana or Charles)
Isla Gardner-by-Floreana
Punta Sur

Isla Española (Hood)
Punta Suárez
Isla Gardner

I search
www.lonelyplanet.com

CONTENTS

INTRODUCTION

WHEN the first naturalists stepped ashore on the Galápagos Islands, they struggled to understand how such an assemblage of diverse and unique wildlife could have occurred on this remote, barren archipelago. Some creatures, such as sea lions and seabirds, were familiar, but others, such as sea-going lizards and tool-using finches, had never been encountered before. Since then the Galápagos Islands and their wildlife have woven their spell on millions of people around the world, thanks to countless documentaries, magazine articles and books. For many wildlife-watchers this is the ultimate experience, not just for the tame animals but also for the sense of occasion, the chance to walk in a living laboratory of evolution. And visiting the Galápagos is easier now than it has ever been for experienced naturalist, curious backpacker and cruise-ship aficionado alike.

The Galápagos Islands are one of the few places left on earth where you can watch wild animals at close range – above and below the sea. This book aims to help you get the most out of your wildlife-watching experience. We've picked out what we consider to be the best sites to visit and described all of the animals you are likely to encounter, with fascinating, easy-to-read information about their biology and how they fit into the unique Galápagos ecosystem. The islands' equatorial climate and rugged terrain present their own challenges, and we've provided tips on how to maximise your comfort and safety. And chances are the animals will be just as curious about you, so this book will help you interpret what you see as you get up close and personal. Information on bird-watching, whale- and dolphin-watching, diving and snorkelling, and wildlife photography will help both beginner and experienced wildlife-watchers.

The Galápagos Islands were known to early explorers as Las Islas Encantadas – Enchanted Isles – and none of that enchantment has been lost down the centuries. Visitors continue to fall under the islands' spell as they step over dozing sea lions to come face-to-face with abundant and tame birdlife and lumbering giant tortoises, all against a background of cactus forests, giant scalesias (tree daisies) and active volcanoes. Yet when Charles Darwin visited in 1835 there were no guidebooks to help piece together the evolutionary puzzle he saw before him. Equipped with *Watching Wildlife Galápagos Islands*, we hope the modern-day visitor will find explanations for the remarkable life forms that first piqued Darwin's curiosity, and continue to show an interest in and support for these unique islands. ■

AUTHOR

David Andrew

David took to wildlife-watching the way some people take to sport or religion. Since the age of five he has wanted to explore the Galápagos Islands but first he needed to arm himself with some credentials. After creating *Wingspan*, Australia's bird-watching magazine, and a spell as editor of *Wildlife Australia*, he instigated Lonely Planet's Watching Wildlife series and has since coauthored *Watching Wildlife Australia, Watching Wildlife East Africa, Watching Wildlife Southern Africa* and *Watching Wildlife Central America*. Nature writing has taken David to some of the world's great wild places, including Papua New Guinea, Borneo and Uganda; and as a scientist he has monitored seabirds and whales in Antarctica, and studied the endangered giant panda in southwest China. Working on *Watching Wildlife Galápagos Islands* left him in no doubt that Charles Darwin was oh so right...

PHOTOGRAPHER

Richard I'Anson is a Melbourne-based travel photographer. His work has been widely published and exhibited around the world, and he travels frequently to photograph both remote and well-known destinations. Lonely Planet has been using Richard's photographs for 15 years and his work has been featured in over 300 editions of LP titles. From the game parks of Southern Africa in search of the Big Five to the jungles of the subcontinent where the elusive tiger roams, Richard has discovered time and again just how hard it is to get close enough to take frame-filling wildlife images. So he reports it was a real pleasure to go to a place where, in some spots, he really did have to be careful not to stand on the wildlife!

FROM THE AUTHOR

Thanks to Brian and Pam Cooke for good company and hospitality in Puerto Ayora; the helpful staff at the Charles Darwin Research Station (CDRS) for letting me loose in their library; Glenys Tuena of the South America Travel Centre in Melbourne for organising my trip to South America and the islands themselves; and Richard I'Anson for taking a great selection of photos. Thanks to all the fellow wildlife enthusiasts I met along the way for their helpful comments about this and other Watching Wildlife guides. And a big thanks to everyone at Lonely Planet who helped to make this book a reality, including Lindsay Brown, Andrew Bain, Marg Toohey and Glenn van der Knijff.

THIS BOOK

Watching Wildlife Galápagos Islands 1 was commissioned and developed in Lonely Planet's Melbourne office by Andrew Bain and Marg Toohey. Publishing managers Lindsay Brown and Chris Rennie oversaw the development of this book. Cartography was overseen by Alison Lyall, and the project was managed by Glenn van der Knijff, with assistance from Fabrice Rocher.

Production was coordinated by Gabbi Wilson (editorial) and Vicki Beale (layout). Editorial assistance was provided by Brooke Lyons and Tegan Murray, and layout assistance was provided by Indra Kilfoyle, Jacqueline McLeod and Wendy Wright. Maps for this guide were drawn by Karen Grant and Andrew Smith, and Wayne Murphy produced the back cover map. The cover was designed by Wendy Wright, and the book was indexed by Gabbi Wilson.

Thanks also to Roslyn Cameron, David Blanton and Desirée Cruz.

INTERNAL PHOTOGRAPHS

All photographs by Richard I'Anson except the following: **David Andrew** 34 top, 88, 125 top; **APL/Corbis/Stephen Frink** 126 bottom; **Chris Beall** 82 top, 107 top, 110 bottom; **Graham Bell** 112 column 1; **Steve Bird** 110 top; **Tom Cockrem** 104 column 2; **Martin Cohen** 120 top; **Juliet Coombe** 40 bottom; **Jason Edwards** 115 top; **Jeff Greenberg** 37 bottom, 57 top; **John Hay** 98 bottom; **Ralph Lee Hopkins** 20, 26 top, 47, 48 top, 52 bottom, 89, 99 bottom, 100 bottom, 102 bottom, 104 column 3, 105 top, 108 bottom, 114 top, 116 column 4; **Greg Johnston** 99 top; **Paul Kennedy** 22; **Ernest Manewal** 36 top, 45 top, 85, 120 bottom, 127 column 1, 2, 3, 4; **Ethan Meleg** 116 inset; **Richard Mills** 112 column 4; **Mark Newman** 76; **David Tipling** 116 column 2; **Wes Walker** 80 bottom, 103 bottom, 104 column 4, 105 bottom.

ACKNOWLEDGMENTS

Many thanks to the following for the use of their content: globe on back cover © Mountain High Maps 1993 Digital Wisdom, Inc.

HOW TO USE THIS BOOK

YOU'RE here to see the animals and we're here to help you: *Watching Wildlife Galápagos Islands* shows you how to recognise the major players and advises you on where to find them. This book is also packed with background information on wildlife habitats, and advice on getting started, when to go and how to prepare. There are also detailed watching tips (eg which trail to hike), and clues on the best time to look. Read on to help plan your wildlife-watching adventure and get the best out of this treasure-trove.

Nature

Wildlife-Watching

Habitats

Islands

Wildlife Gallery

Each chapter is colour coded to help you navigate through the book – look for the thumb tabs.

Getting Started There are two main ways to go about watching wildlife: pick your animals and then find out where to go; or choose where you want to go and then find out what's there. In the Galápagos you'll see some wildlife in a lot of places (eg the seabird colonies on Genovesa); but for other animals you'll need to go to certain places (eg the highlands of Santa Cruz for giant tortoises). The key chapters cover both approaches: Islands describes where to go and what's there, and the Wildlife Gallery tells you about the animals. Flipping between these chapters will tell you almost everything you need to know.

Table of Contents This gives you a quick overview of the book. We've colour-coded each chapter to help you find your way around until you're more familiar with the layout.

Nature in the Galápagos Islands We explain the reasons behind the Galápagos Islands' great biodiversity and introduce some of the conservation issues.

Wildlife-Watching Essential background reading, this chapter tells you when to go and how to look, and explains all the ins and outs of tours, guides, equipment and field guides. Special features cover bird-watching, whale- and dolphin-watching, diving and snorkelling, and wildlife photography.

Habitats Describes the ecosystems of the Galápagos in simple terms.

Wildlife-Watching

Islands Tour itineraries differ between companies and from season to season, and each island has its own different attractions. Therefore, we've started this chapter with the main gateway, Puerto Ayora. After that, the islands appear roughly in order of their proximity to Puerto Ayora, starting with Santa Cruz (on which Puerto Ayora is located). Islands that have many attractions and visitor sites, such as Isabela, are given detailed treatment over several pages. Other islands, such as Santa Fé, which many people visit as a day trip, may be covered in one page only. At the end of this chapter is a section about the Charles Darwin Research Station (CDRS) in Puerto Ayora.

Facts for travellers (such as location, facilities, accommodation, contacts and photo opportunities), watching tips and wildlife highlights are summarised for each island, and a colour map points out major features and good wildlife-viewing areas.

Wildlife Gallery This is a rundown of all the key species and groups: what they look like (and how to tell them apart) and the kinds of things you can see them doing. Coloured thumb tabs divide this chapter into three broad groupings: mammals, birds and other creatures, such as reptiles.

Key animals are presented as feature pages, which describe unusual and interesting aspects of their ecology. A sidebar next to the main text summarises some of their main characteristics (eg habitat, behaviour, breeding), and a Hotspots box lists some of the places where they might be found (use this as a link to the Islands chapter). Other animals appear in family groups (eg Darwin's finches) or are grouped according to the habitat in which they are found (eg marine life) – these pages are packed with photos to help you work out what's what.

Islands

Wildlife highlights

General island information

Island map

Watching tips

Wildlife Gallery

Group page

Highlight page

Hotspots: where to find animals

Summary information

Resource Guide Lists recommended field guides and other books, reliable tour operators, and wildlife-related websites.

Glossary Explains any confusing or unfamiliar words that appear in the text.

Index The quickest way to find out about an animal or a particular island is to look it up in the Index. Animals are arranged into groups according to their common names (eg 'blue-footed booby' can be found under 'booby'), and page numbers in bold indicate a photo of that animal. Islands are listed alphabetically by name.

ECOTOURISM

BE it exploring the rainforests of Brazil or diving Australia's Great Barrier Reef, the urge to experience the globe's pristine places is strong for many travellers. But while verdant jungles and stunning seascapes delight, for the majority they are just a glorious backdrop – what they have really come to see is the wildlife. From tracking chimpanzees in Uganda to spotting whales in the Bahamas, seeing the world's most famous wildlife has become a popular international pastime. Since their East African beginnings in the 1970s, nature tours have gone global and they are now a significant source of revenue for many developing and developed countries. Today's nature tour hotspots include East and Southern Africa, Australia, Nepal, Thailand, Alaska, the Amazon Basin, Central America and, of course, the Galápagos Islands.

'Ecotourism' takes the concept of a nature tour and pushes it one step further. The essence of ecotourism is not only about seeing and interacting with nature, it's also about doing so in a way that preserves and sustains it. At its simplest, you are helping conservation merely by paying park entrance fees. For example, nearly half of your US$100 Galápagos National Park (GNP) entry fee is channelled back into the park, helping to ensure its ongoing protection. But more than that, genuine ecotourism ensures that the people living in and around those parks also benefit, and so have a vested interest in conserving nature and wildlife. The trained guides who accompany every tour in the Galápagos Islands are local people who have come to appreciate that the archipelago's wildlife is far more valuable – and sustainable – as a living resource than it would be if exploited for other purposes. Ecotourism in the Galápagos guarantees jobs and an improved lifestyle, not just for guides, but for the host of people involved in maintaining the infrastructure and services of the islands' gateways.

Ecotourism or Egotourism?

To ensure that you help rather than hinder the wildlife and places you visit, do a little research. A starting point is the recommended list of tour operators on p130, and you might also ask the following questions. Does the company:

- Employ local people and use local products and services?
- Make contributions to the Galápagos National Park (GNP)?
- Sponsor local environmental projects?
- Keep tour-group numbers small to reduce impact on the environment and local cultures?
- Aid environmental and wildlife researchers?
- Educate travellers about wildlife, the environment and local cultures?

Ecotour operators offer an incredible variety of tours and contribute to the principles of ecotourism in a number of different ways. Don't expect a 'yes' to each of the above questions, but if you get a 'no' to every one, ask the company to explain in detail how it contributes to ecotourism; if the answer doesn't satisfy you, consider looking further afield.

Ecotourism in the Galápagos Islands

The name 'Galápagos' is probably identified with unique wildlife more than any other destination on earth, and when you visit this unique archipelago you are a participant in ecotourism. A set of guidelines has been developed for the protection of Galápagos National Park (GNP) and it is in everyone's interests that these rules are followed. For a full list of guidelines, visit the website of the **International Galápagos Tour Operators Association** (IGTOA; www.igtoa.org/info_for_travelers/park_rules.php), but in particular, remember that: you must remain on marked trails and within designated visitor areas; it is forbidden to remove any live or dead plant or animal material from the islands, and to transport these to or between the islands; animals must never be touched, fed, chased or otherwise disturbed (this goes for nests, eggs and babies as well); and all litter must be left on the boat or taken off the islands when you leave. Your tour guides are dedicated to protecting this unique environment and will strictly enforce these rules if necessary. And, generally speaking, the rules designed for the protection of GNP can be applied to every ecotourism destination on earth, so it is a good idea to be familiar with them. In addition, when buying souvenirs, ensure that they are not made from endangered plants and animals, or parts thereof.

Today, ecotourism is probably tourism's fastest-growing sector, and although not everyone who travels to nature hotspots wishes to see *only* wildlife, it is almost certain they will visit a national park or reserve for some wildlife-watching while they are there. Unfortunately, the rising popularity of ecotours (fuelled by increasing international publicity about the environment and concern for its demise) has led to flamboyant misuse of the term among tour operators seeking profit. Brochures and websites abound with the label, but many organisations are eco-sensitive in name only; at worst they exhibit the greatest failings of the tourist industry, ultimately destroying the places they tout through overdevelopment and exploitation of local people and wildlife. Fortunately there are many tour operators that offer the real thing. There are also a variety of organisations (including the UN and international conservation and human rights groups) working to promote guidelines and standards for ecotour operators and monitor their activities. For tips on choosing an ecotour company, see the boxed text opposite.

And don't forget, wherever you are, to make your own eco-contributions: respect local cultures, avoid disturbing wildlife and don't buy wildlife products (unless they are legal and encourage conservation of the resource). For more tips, see p32. More so than at any other time in history, travellers today have the incredible wealth of life on earth at their fingertips; there is almost nowhere on the planet that is truly inaccessible and, theoretically at least, no wild species that cannot be viewed and enjoyed. Equally though, many of the charismatic animals that tourists wish to see are facing extinction within the next century. By undertaking travel that adheres to the principles of ecotourism, you, the traveller, are helping to prevent that. ■

NATURE IN THE GALÁPAGOS ISLANDS

*An Introduction to the Galápagos Islands'
Natural History*

ENVIRONMENT

Lava cactus growing in pahoehoe lava below Volcán La Cumbre, Fernandina. Such 'pioneer' plants create microhabitats in which soil and moisture accumulate, allowing other plants to become established.

Previous page: A candelabra cactus blooming in Puerto Baquerizo Moreno, San Cristóbal.

Shaped by Fire & Water

Isolated by vast stretches of the Pacific Ocean, the Galápagos archipelago straddles the equator 1000km west of South America and sits entirely within the tropics. The many islands that make up the archipelago range in size from the largest, 130km-long Isabela, to the numerous islets and rocks that sit only a few metres above sea level. The entire area is volcanic in origin and the main islands are the tips of vast submarine volcanoes, some now weathered and extinct but others, such as Fernandina and Isabela, among the most active volcanic areas on earth. In 1968 Fernandina's caldera floor plummeted 350m, and as this book was going to press Volcán La Cumbre erupted again. Volcán Cerro Azul on Isabela erupted as recently as 1998, and uplifts continue to reshape coastlines. No island appears to be more than five million years old and the newest are less than a million years old. Fernandina, one of the youngest, is the largest pristine island on earth, with no human habitation or introduced animals or plants. Evidence of volcanic activity, such as lava flows and cratered tuff cones, can be seen everywhere, although a few islands, such as Santa Fé, are slabs of basaltic rock uplifted from the sea floor.

Equatorial climates usually show little seasonal variation, but complex oceanic currents around the Galápagos Islands drive weather and rainfall patterns into two recognisable seasons that influence vegetation and wildlife. Exact timings vary, but the warm waters of the Niño Flow move south in December or January, causing a rise in air temperature and the build-up of large cumulus clouds around the islands. The 'warm' season lasts until about May and this is when 90% of the annual rain falls, especially over the high islands. By April the southeast trade winds start to push the Humboldt Current north from the coast of Peru, and a cooler, dry season that sets in by June lasts for the rest of the year. The Humboldt's cool, rich waters bring vast food resources to the Galápagos and seabird colonies reach their peak of activity in the dry. Precipitation in the cooler months most often takes the form of a light, misty rain known as garúa.

El Niño

Every year a little-understood climatic phenomenon, named El Niño (Child) after the Christ child because it often arrives around Christmas time, brings warm surface water to the coasts of Peru and Ecuador, affecting the Galápagos irregularly but on average every seven years. Heavy rains favour land animals and plants, but the warm water depresses fish numbers and thus affects breeding seabirds and sea lions. And a big El Niño, such as occurred in 1982–83 and 1997–98, can be disastrous for all life forms. Sea temperatures can reach 30°C, altering the species composition of seaweed and sending fish to great depths in search of cool waters where seabirds and sea lions can't reach them. In 1982–83 marine iguanas starved en masse and up to half the seabird and sea lion populations perished. Even terrestrial wildlife was affected: cacti became so waterlogged in the massive rainfall they collapsed under their own weight and finch numbers exploded only to collapse again in the ensuing dry when food supplies ran out.

However, rainfall varies from place to place and year to year. More rain falls on high islands than low ones, and more falls at high altitude than sea level. The northern sides of islands lie in the rain shadow of prevailing southeasterly winds and consequently receive less rain than the southern side of the same island. In some years, heavy rains begin in late December and last until May; in other years there may be nothing more than a few light showers for the entire wet season. The heaviest and most extensive rains fall during El Niño years.

From Rocky Barrens to Lush Peaks

In the short span of geological time since the various islands were formed, they have been transformed from barren, sterile lava flows into complex vegetation communities with many unique species. Known as succession, the process can take millennia, although it often happens much more quickly, depending on factors such as climate, geology and rainfall; it continues all over the islands today. Thus, a visitor can step ashore onto brittle, barely cooled lava and see pioneering lava cactus and mangroves at the sea's edge. Both eventually change conditions enough on the soil for other, less specialised plants to take hold, and a few metres inland progressively richer soils support bands of distinctive vegetation that climax in the dense greenery of the highlands. Terrestrial plant communities change in composition with altitude and can be broadly divided into the arid, transitional and moist zones; the moist zone is usually further divided into three or four categories (see p54). The number of zones found on each island depends on its elevation and therefore climate. All of the small islands and the lowlands of the larger islands are covered by the arid zone, but moist forest grows only on high islands such as Santa Cruz, Isabela and Floreana; on some islands, much of the fertile moist zone has been cleared.

A large percentage of the flora has affinities with that of tropical South and Central America, and some species resemble plants that now occur only in the West Indies. The first plant colonists were most probably tiny seeds light enough to be carried by the wind and some 30% of species appear to have arrived in this way. About 60% of all species were carried to the islands by birds, either stuck to their feet or feathers, or ingested as food elsewhere and deposited with their droppings, and the rest drifted by sea. Approximately 750 species of vascular plant have been catalogued to date in the Galápagos, and new species and subspecies are still being described. More than 540 species are indigenous and of these 170 are endemic; nearly 200 are weeds or plants introduced by humans.

Some land plants are almost as distinctive as the well-known animals and, like them, show excellent examples of adaptive radiation (see No Situations Vacant, p18). Of particular note are the 20 species of scalesia, the so-called tree daisies, which vary from small shrubs to 15m-tall woody trees that grow in dense stands akin to cloud forest. The six species of opuntia cactus (prickly pear) have coevolved with animals as varied as cactus-finches, carpenter bees and land iguanas, and have also radiated into diverse forms. ∎

Surfing the Hot Spot

Tectonic plates are huge slabs of the earth's crust that slide and usually collide imperceptibly (although sometimes with cataclysmic force) over the molten magma in the earth's core. The Galápagos sit on the Nazca plate, which is moving towards South America. The islands themselves are the tips of huge submarine volcanoes, formed where the superheated magma pierces the crust at a hot spot or mantle plume. The Galápagos hot spot is about 150km wide, and because it remains stationary, the Nazca plate effectively 'surfs' over it as it moves east. Thus, the western islands are the youngest, the eastern islands are the oldest and the Carnegie Ridge, a series of submerged sea mountains halfway between the Galápagos and South America, are probably the ancient, eroded stumps of even older islands.

WILDLIFE

A captive giant tortoise at the Charles Darwin Research Station (CDRS) in Puerto Ayora, Santa Cruz. The tortoises' ancestors probably drifted to the archipelago from mainland South America and, in the absence of competition from other grazers, evolved to their great size.

Castaways & Colonists

The Galápagos Islands have never been connected to South America and emerged from the Pacific Ocean as a result of volcanic activity at various times during the past few million years. Clearly the wildlife, especially the land vertebrates, couldn't have appeared spontaneously on the barren lava flows. They had to come from somewhere else. And it is patently obvious that the modern animal inhabitants are closely related to similar animals in South and Central America. So how did they get to the Galápagos across 1000km of ocean?

During the wet season great clumps of vegetation – whole trees, in fact – are torn from the banks of great rivers in flood and washed out to sea. This phenomenon can still be seen each year in Ecuador's Guaya River, which empties in the direction of the Galápagos. The small animals that live in or on this erstwhile terrestrial vegetation (mainly invertebrates but also reptiles and small mammals) must cling to it for survival when the deluge strikes. But what happens next is a matter of chance and timing. Many are washed far out to sea and of course perish, but those that survive dehydration, starvation and predation may eventually fetch up on an uninhabited shore. In fact, it is well documented that animals can colonise islands on 'rafts' of vegetation and this phenomenon sets a highly feasible scene for the invasion of the Galápagos archipelago by land animals.

But only certain groups, such as rodents and reptiles, are small, tough and adaptable enough to survive such an epic crossing, and to do so in sufficient numbers to found a viable colony. Thus, amphibians, which cannot survive long without fresh water to maintain their metabolism, never became established in the Galápagos (until recently – see A Short Hop to Disaster, p78). The species that did prosper evolved into comparatively few endemic forms because of the demanding environmental conditions.

Terrestrial mammals are the least diverse group of vertebrates in the Galápagos: if any other forms survived the crossing from the mainland – and South America is rich in land mammals – only rodents became established, radiating into at least seven species of rice rat. But, of course, the Pacific was no barrier to bats and

No Situations Vacant

Adaptive radiation is the process whereby several species evolve from a common ancestor over a relatively short period of evolutionary time to fill available ecological niches. Most famous are the Darwin's finches, whose common ancestor evolved into 13 species, each able to exploit different feeding niches with their unique bill shape and size; thus, the warbler finch flits and gleans among foliage for insects, the large ground-finch crushes stout seeds and the cactus-finch probes opuntia blossoms. But textbook examples of this phenomenon crop up repeatedly in the Galápagos. For example, 65 endemic species of land and freshwater snail each occupy separate microhabitats from sea level to the damp highlands. And the 20 species of scalesia (tree daisy) range from small arid-zone shrubs to 15m-tall woody trees that replace forest trees in the highlands. And the process continues: the blood-drinking, so-called vampire-finches of Islas Darwin and Wolf are actually sharp-beaked ground-finches that could yet become specialised into a full species.

marine mammals, such as cetaceans (whales and dolphins) and pinnipeds (sea lions and relatives). Some 25 species of cetacean have been recorded in the Galápagos; some appear to be resident (bottlenose dolphins and Bryde's whales) or are regular visitors (sperm whales), while others are known from only a single, beach-cast specimen. And deserted islands suit pinnipeds just fine: the Galápagos sea lion is descended from the wide-ranging California sea lion and the Galápagos fur seal most probably colonised the tropics from the subantarctic via the cold Humboldt Current.

Hardy Survivors & Waves of Invaders

Reptiles are great survivors and the Galápagos are unusual for a wildlife destination in having several high-profile species. The green sea turtle is abundant and nests on deserted beaches; and, apart from a few species of snake and small lizard, there are large land iguanas, a unique marine iguana and the famous giant tortoise. Giant tortoises obviously couldn't cling to rafts of vegetation, but they can survive for months on their backs, even floating on the sea – and in any case the ancestral tortoise probably wasn't a giant. Related species in South America are much smaller and probably attained great size after arriving in the Galápagos because there were no competing animals to stop them.

However, small animals can spread by other means. For example, a veritable plankton of spider hatchlings and small insects drifts constantly on air currents thousands of metres above the earth's surface, settling by chance on land far from their origin. Others, such as tiny snails (or their eggs), can be transported in mud on waterbirds' legs. And, of course, birds are inveterate colonists, able to migrate for vast distances across open sea.

The bird tally in the Galápagos stands at about 140, including 28 endemic species and 16 endemic subspecies (many of which could be reclassified as full species pending further research). Many are nonbreeding visitors, such as migratory waders and waterfowl, and additional vagrants turn up nearly every year. Breeding seabirds are abundant and diverse, particularly the pelicans and allies; others, such as the waved albatross and Galápagos penguin, are tropical anomalies among families normally found in high latitudes; and the flightless cormorant is simply unique. But the arid climate allowed the establishment of only a few waterbirds, and the land birds that became established were invariably generalists and opportunists, such as Galápagos hawks. The ancestor of the most famous avian inhabitants, the 13 species of Darwin's finch, radiated to fill most available feeding niches, precluding the establishment of many other small species.

Animals without backbones are comparatively little-studied, but more than 2250 species of land and freshwater invertebrate have so far been recorded, of which more than 50% are endemic. The inhabitants of Galápagos waters show affinities with marine faunas of the Pacific, Atlantic and Caribbean; some 400 species of fish have been recorded, of which 10% are endemic.

Since the arrival of humans, a new suite of invaders has appeared, transported by ship, deliberately introduced by people, and as hitchhikers on exotic plants and animals – consequences for endemic and native wildlife have often been disastrous. ▪

Measuring Biodiversity
For all practical purposes, the species is the fundamental biological unit and biodiversity is measured in species richness. But natural ecosystems are always changing and in a numbers-obsessed world definitive species counts are difficult to come by; species disappear and new ones are constantly being discovered or recognised by further research. For example, a new species of scalesia (tree daisy) was discovered in 1985; the Santiago rice rat, long thought to be extinct, was rediscovered in 1997; and the Charles Darwin Research Station (CDRS) announced in 2003 that the Galápagos sea lion, long regarded as a subspecies of the California sea lion, is actually a distinct species. Understanding the full species richness of the Galápagos is still a long way off, and is a full-time job for researchers.

HUMANS & WILDLIFE

An inquisitive Galápagos sea-lion pup nibbling a visitor's toes. Such encounters must always be on the animal's terms and wild animals in the Galápagos must never be handled.

Malice in Wonderland

Until about 500 years ago – a heartbeat in evolutionary time – the wildlife of the Galápagos Islands was oblivious to the existence of humans. But with the advent of long-distance sea travel, it was only a matter of time before humans stepped ashore. Some historians believe the first visitors may have been Incas on balsa rafts in the 1400s, but the first written record was in 1535, when a Spaniard, Thomas de Berlanga, noted '…seals, turtles and such big tortoises that each could carry a man on top of itself, and many iguanas that are like serpents…'

Oceanic islands typically support few terrestrial predators so birds commonly evolve flightlessness and other wildlife is often tame. But this blissful state has an often fatal corollary: 'ecological naivety', whereby wildlife fails to recognise a new threat, such as humans and their animal servants. Thus, archipelagos such as Hawaii and New Zealand suffered waves of extinctions soon after the arrival of primitive humans, and the age of sail heralded the rampant exploitation of the Galápagos' tame wildlife.

De Berlanga's impact was minimal, but from the 16th century onwards an ever-increasing stream of buccaneers and other seafarers used various sites around the islands to replenish their supplies. High on their list of priorities was fresh meat, and giant tortoises were ideal for long voyages: they were defenceless against humans, could be stored alive on their backs for months on end and were available in apparently inexhaustible numbers. From an estimated 200,000 their population crashed to as low as 15,000 over three centuries. And exploitation did not stop with these defenceless reptiles. The abundant whales in Galápagos waters were hunted relentlessly, as everywhere, from the 1790s until the late 19th century; and fur seals were hunted almost to extinction for their luxurious pelts right up to the 1930s.

By the time the killing had stopped, some of the livestock and vermin that accompany people everywhere had run wild over the islands. They remain one of the most pernicious problems facing wildlife conservation in the Galápagos to this day. Goats were released to breed on many islands to ensure a constant supply of fresh meat for passing vessels; and pigs, donkeys and

Honouring the Great Man

In 1959, the centenary of the publication of *The Origin of Species*, the Charles Darwin Foundation was founded to further the conservation of Galápagos ecosystems. The Charles Darwin Research Station (CDRS; p91) was built next to Bahía Academy in Puerto Ayora on Santa Cruz in 1964. It now has a team of more than 200 scientists, educators, volunteers, students and staff dedicated to scientific research and environmental education. Their broad brief includes the monitoring and control of invasive species, marine research, restoring the population of giant tortoises, land iguanas and opuntias, and public education. The CDRS is open to the public daily and features giant tortoise and land iguana breeding corrals, an interpretive centre, a library and a shop. There's another giant tortoise breeding facility at Puerto Villamil on Isabela and environmental education centres on Isabela and San Cristóbal. A visit to the CDRS is highly recommended and the excellent Charles Darwin Foundation website (www.darwinfoundation.org) features news, updates and background information.

cattle escaped domesticity to roam feral. Rats ran ashore from the holds of ships, and feral populations of companion animals, such as cats and dogs, also became established. These intelligent, efficient and adaptable killers remain a serious pest on some islands, and feral hoofed animals in vast numbers continue to destroy natural vegetation and soils.

A Brighter Future

Luckily, the challenging climate and shortage of potable water made it difficult for humans to become permanently established on the islands. Even today only Santa Cruz, San Cristóbal, Floreana and Isabela have human residents. Nonetheless, large tracts of natural forest in the highlands were cleared for cattle-grazing, agriculture and the planting of food crops. 'Domestic' plants ran wild as weeds (some, such as quinine, have become a serious threat to native vegetation) and insect pests (such as fire ants) arrived unwelcome on exotic vegetation. A small fishing industry sprang up in Puerto Villamil on Isabela, but various enterprises, such as moss-gathering, fish canneries and salt-mining, all proved unsustainable and the tiny population barely eked out a living.

After Charles Darwin's visit and the publication of *The Origin of Species* in 1859, the islands came under increasing scrutiny from scientific bodies. And a major expedition by the California Academy of Sciences in 1906 helped focus the attention of both scientists and the public on the archipelago. After a Unesco assessment in 1957 the Ecuadorian government became convinced that the Galápagos' unique natural state was better preserved intact, and in 1959 the Galápagos National Park (GNP) was declared (p23), paving the way for intensive research and conservation programs, and the then-unheard-of ecotourism industry.

Mass tourism began in 1970 and from humble beginnings has become the biggest industry on the islands, peaking at 60,000 visitors a year. The impact of tourists at the well-regulated visitor sites is probably minimal, but even ecofriendly tourists need food, accommodation, transport and infrastructure. The permanent population has burgeoned to meet these needs; impoverished Ecuadorians flock to the islands seeking comparatively well-paid employment and the official population grew from 2000 in 1960 to about 17,000 at the beginning of the 21st century. Collectively, the impact is enormous: the Galápagos have a serious waste-disposal problem, housing construction pushes further into natural habitat and cargo ships ply the waters daily, increasing the risk of wrecks and oil spills. Tourism operators constantly lobby for bigger and better ships and hotels, and for the Galápagos National Park Service (GNPS) to open yet more visitor sites.

Meanwhile, factory-ships fish illegally in Galápagos waters for tuna and sharks; and high prices tempt Puerto Villamil's small fishing fleet to poach sea cucumbers, known locally as *pepinos,* for the Asian market (see p49). Under intense pressure, the GNPS struck an accord allowing the sustainable harvest of *pepinos,* but the long-term effects of this industry remain to be seen.

With worldwide publicity through documentaries, articles and books, the Galápagos seems assured its place in the sun. If the current policies of sustainable and responsible tourism continue, its pristine nature should prevail. ■

The Wreck of the Jessica
On the night of 16 January 2001 the *Jessica,* a tanker carrying 240,000 gallons of oil, grounded on the coast of San Cristóbal and one of the worst fears of conservationists was realised. Attempts to right the stricken vessel failed and oil started to leak into the surrounding waters within days. Sea lions, marine iguanas, gulls and boobies were treated for oiling, but thanks to a swift and coordinated response from volunteers, fishermen and local and international institutes, the effects of the disaster were less than expected. Even so, the cleanup has so far cost in excess of US$2.3 million, and with an increasing number of ships plying Galápagos waters a serious spill remains a constant threat.

CONSERVATION

Galápagos sea lions resting on a fishing boat in Puerto Baquerizo Moreno, San Cristóbal. Conflict between the fishing industry and conservationists has been a source of friction on some islands.

Rescue & Restoration

Compared to, say, Hawaii or Mauritius, the Galápagos have suffered a short tally of extinctions, but only Fernandina, Genovesa, Darwin, Wolf and the smaller islands have escaped completely the destructive effects of humans and introduced animals. Since European seafarers first set foot on the Galápagos, three species of rice rat are known to have become extinct and a species of gecko may also be extinct. Three subspecies of giant tortoise have disappeared, and the last survivor of the distinct Pinta subspecies, Lonesome George, is biologically extinct, even if he lives for another 50 years, because he is a male.

Species ebb and flow over the course of evolutionary time, and owing to the very nature of the islands many animals and plants live a precarious existence; some, such as the mangrove finch, were probably always rare. And variations in marine productivity can threaten the survival of seabirds and pinnipeds during major El Niño events, which can lead to total breeding failure and/or starvation in some species. Wildlife appears to recover quickly from such natural perturbations, and background extinctions, a natural process whereby a species evolves and becomes extinct over millions of years, have occurred since the beginning of time (although they have been greatly accelerated by recent human activity). However, there's no room for complacency and a major manmade disaster, such as an oil spill, could be the deciding factor that tips the scales against the survival of several key species.

The control of introduced animals and plants remains the highest (and most expensive) priority for the CDRS and GNPS. Feral goats continue to affect sensitive giant tortoise habitat on northern Isabela; elephant grass is choking out native plants, such as Darwin's daisy, in the Santa Cruz highlands; and feral pigs continue to affect the breeding success of sea turtles and greater flamingos. The list goes on, and as planes and boats continue to import invertebrate pests that could potentially devastate wildlife of all sizes, even monitoring their spread is a huge task.

It's not all bad news, of course, and the GNPS and CDRS have run very successful captive-breeding programs for giant tortoises and land iguanas in tandem with pest-control and habitat-restoration programs. Since 1965, more than 2500 giant tortoises

Public Enemy Number One, Two, Three...

The list of vertebrate animals deliberately introduced to the Galápagos that have since become pests includes dogs, cats, pigs, cattle, donkeys and horses. But public enemy number one is the goat, which, after humans, is probably the most destructive animal on earth. Eradication campaigns have been very successful on Española, Rábida, Santa Fé and South Plaza, but these pests remain a huge problem on Isabela, where an estimated 100,000 roam the slopes of volcanoes and destroy giant tortoise habitat. Their control is difficult, time-consuming and expensive, and eradication will take years; and there are other factors to consider, like how to dispose of thousands of corpses. Simultaneous pest-control campaigns in various parts of the archipelago are tackling pigs, dogs, cats and rats where they are a major problem, and smooth-billed anis are also being targeted because of their impact on native birds. Unfortunately new pests, animal and plant, are constantly arriving.

have been repatriated to Española, Pinzón, Santa Cruz and Santiago, 1000 of them to Española alone. The land iguana program started in 1976, when wild dogs had all but wiped them out on Santa Cruz; to date more than 750 adults and juveniles have been repatriated at various sites and now breed in the wild.

Planning for the Future

The Galápagos National Park (GNP) was declared by the Ecuadorian government in 1959 to protect all parts of the archipelago except those already occupied or farmed by people, and in 1979 the islands were declared a World Heritage Site by Unesco. The CDRS was opened in 1964 (see Honouring the Great Man, p20) and the GNPS was set up in 1968 to oversee the running of the park. The GNPS works closely with the CDRS to implement conservation and research programs, and to plan the sustainable use of the islands. For example, visitor sites were established on most islands to meet and mitigate the growing demands of tourists. All visitors to the Galápagos must now be accompanied by a licensed Galápagos naturalist guide and remain on designated trails or within visitor sites. Guides are included as crew members on all tour vessels to interpret the natural and human history, and to enforce GNPS regulations.

Currently, the GNP is managed by a system of five integrated zones that recognise the needs of both humans and wildlife. High Protective Zones, such as Fernandina, are pristine areas with absolute protection; Primitive Zones make up most of the park and have restricted access; Special Use Zones are considerably altered from their natural state and abut population centres; Visitor Zones are set aside for extensive, intensive or recreational use; and External Zones are areas outside GNP, such as farming and urban areas. In 1986 a presidential decree established the Galápagos Marine Resources Reserve, which included the waters surrounding the islands to a distance of 15 nautical miles – a total area of some 70,000 sq km. And in 2002 the lagoons near Puerto Villamil on Isabela were recognised by the Ramsar Convention as Wetlands of International Importance.

In 1998 a new law addressing the main issues of Galápagos conservation was ratified, specifically extending the marine reserve to 40 nautical miles offshore and outlawing industrial fishing. But the small fishing industry based in Puerto Villamil continues to be a thorn in the side of conservationists. After decimating the lobster population, the industry turned its attention to the lucrative Asian sea cucumber market. After poached catches and illegal processing camps were raided by GNPS personnel, the fishermen turned violent, committing atrocities against wildlife and assaulting GNPS staff. Eventually an accord was struck, with the fishermen allowed a strictly controlled annual harvest of *pepinos*.

Several international organisations help fund research and conservation in the Galápagos, and there are other bodies through which you might be able to pursue volunteer opportunities (see p131). The problems facing the Galápagos are not insurmountable; these remarkable islands attract high-calibre researchers and volunteers who drive enlightened and forward-thinking conservation policies. ■

Six Degrees of Separation

International conservation bodies recognise five different stages before a species becomes extinct. Animals that are insufficiently known are regarded as **data deficient**. Unfortunately, studies often discover cause for concern, and the waved albatross, Galápagos (wedge-rumped) storm-petrel, Galápagos rail and medium tree-finch are known well enough to be classified as **near-threatened**. It's downhill from there: **vulnerable** (which applies to the Galápagos penguin, flightless cormorant, Galápagos hawk and lava gull) indicates a high risk of extinction in the medium term, and **endangered** (the Charles mockingbird and mangrove finch) means that those species face a high risk of extinction in the short term if current trends continue. Just before the point of no return, a species is said to be **critically endangered**; in the Galápagos Islands the dark-rumped petrel wins this dubious accolade.

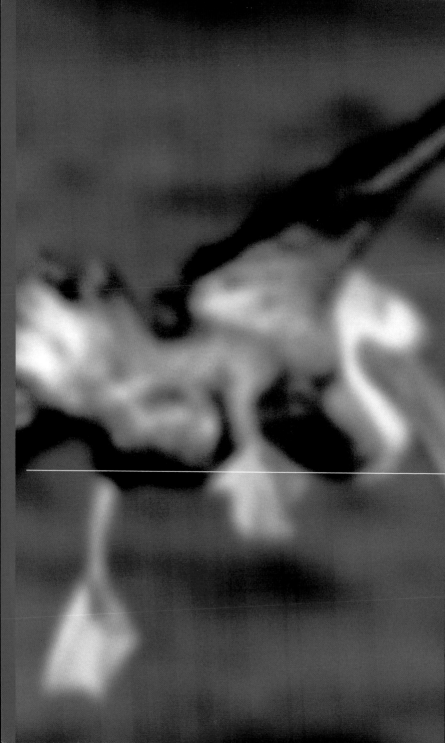

WILDLIFE-WATCHING

*Tips & Hints on the Art
of Watching Wildlife*

WHEN TO GO

A juvenile waved albatross moulting into adult plumage at Punta Suárez, Española. To see these magnificent seabirds your trip will have to coincide with their breeding season (April to December).

Inset: Juvenile Nazca booby at Punta Suárez, Española.

Previous page: A brown pelican in flight, Isla Lobos, San Cristóbal.

Garúa

The annual influx of the Humboldt Current brings cool waters that cause an air temperature inversion around the islands, trapping a layer of thin cloud at an altitude of 500m to 1000m. Known as *garúa*, it can reduce visibility at sea and cloaks mountainsides in a lingering mist that falls as light drizzle, watering the lush greenery of the highlands.

THE Galápagos archipelago lies entirely within the tropics and straddles the equator, so 'normal' seasonal labels don't apply here and there is no 'off' season for travel. Instead, seasonal change is driven by shifts in prevailing winds and oceanic currents (see p16), which in turn change rainfall and temperature patterns. At latitude zero there are no cyclones or hurricanes and with a few notable exceptions, wildlife is present and visible year-round.

A wet season lasting from January to April has average daily temperatures ranging from 22°C to 31°C (70°F to 84°F) and occasional heavy showers or thunderstorms, especially in the afternoon. The wet season usually means calm seas, clear skies (unless it's raining) and warmer water for snorkelling; there's a flush of green over the landscape and for many animals breeding is in full swing. If travelling at this time, be prepared for occasional wet conditions anywhere, on land or sea, although chances are you'll dry off and warm up quickly once a shower passes (remember to keep your camera and other optical equipment dry). And although it is usually hot inland, there's often a pleasant breeze at coastal sites.

The dry season generally lasts from June to November, and features slightly cooler nights and days with average daily temperatures ranging from 19°C to 27°C (68°F to 82°F). The dry is also characterised by the *garúa* and is pleasantly warm, but hazy skies can make conditions less suitable for photography, water is cold for snorkelling at most sites, and seas can be rough at times. On the positive side, many seabirds, including waved albatrosses, congregate to breed in noisy colonies because the seas are rich in food resources.

May and December are the months of transition between the seasons. The exception to the seasonal rainfall pattern is the highlands of large islands, such as Santa Cruz and San Cristóbal,

which can experience rain and mist virtually year-round. A visit to the highlands is usually most productive in the early morning before cloud builds up.

Rainfall in the Galápagos varies greatly from island to island and year to year, but during an El Niño event (p16) it increases dramatically and thunderstorms can occur at any time of day. El Niño events can greatly increase the breeding success of land animals, such as birds, but can also have a disastrous effect on populations of seabirds and mammals such as sea lions.

Most people visit the Galápagos during the Christmas holiday break (December to January) and the northern summer (June to August), and at these times hotels and cruises can be heavily booked and prices correspondingly higher. At other times, passenger numbers can be down considerably and you may find your trip is more intimate and enjoyable as a result. ∎

HOW TO LOOK

Looking at the Right Time & Place

Visitors are often amazed at the apparent ease with which professional guides locate and identify their quarry. But while many years of experience may be the key in some of the world's wildlife destinations, the Galápagos Islands are probably unique in that most animals are easily located and apparently unafraid. There are some exceptions of course and despite this big attraction, some general tips will enhance your wildlife-viewing experience.

A guide talking to tourists at Tagus Cove, Isabela. The guides that accompany every tour of the islands are knowledgable in many aspects of the islands' natural and human history.

Time of Day This is possibly the most important factor determining animal behaviour. Dawn and late afternoon are the most productive periods for the majority of birds; they are the coolest parts of the day and also produce the richest light for photos. By the middle of the day small birds have usually sought respite from the heat, but this is when frigatebirds 'thermal', and when most reptiles are at the peak of their activity. Because visitors aren't allowed onto uninhabited islands at night, you won't get much chance to look for nocturnal animals, but around the streetlights in towns look for bats and night herons hunting small animals.

Weather Intrinsically linked to time of day are the prevailing weather conditions. Heavy rain drives many animals into cover and in such conditions you would need to search sheltered areas, such as crevices in cliffs, the lee of boulders and under dense foliage. But showers can also stimulate the hatching of insects, which in turn attract predators such as lava lizards and flycatchers. Overcast conditions may promote hunting by normally crepuscular predators such as owls, and extremely wet nights might see nocturnal species still active at dawn because they were forced to shelter during their normal activity period. Calm, sunny days are best for seeing snakes and lava lizards.

Water Much Galápagos wildlife is adapted to an arid environment; freshwater pools are a rarity (except at a few sites in the highlands) and are nonexistent on some islands except after rain. However, most birds drink daily when water is available and pools are worthwhile places to invest time. Birds will also readily exploit artificial water sources, and the drinking pools in the CDRS giant tortoise pens are often thronged with finches and mockingbirds.

Food Sources Knowing what your quarry eats will help you decide where to spend time. For instance, flowering opuntias are a magnet for cactus-finches and carpenter bees, and also attract mockingbirds, Galápagos doves and a host of smaller insects. Land iguanas eat the cactus pads and commonly stake out their turf near a productive prickly pear.

Habitat Knowing which habitats are preferred by each species is a good beginning, but just as important is knowing where to look in those habitats. Animals seek out specific sites for shelter, food and so on, and each species has its preference. For example, owls roost

Trail Etiquette

The marked walking trails at each visitor site are designed to let you get the most out of the wildlife there without trampling vegetation or disturbing animals. Apart from a few beaches, visitors must stick to the trails at all times; this regulation is strictly enforced by Galápagos National Park (GNP) authorities and it is vital to obey your guide's instructions. And remember there are other people here too; keep noise to a minimum, especially if you are at the front of the line, and rotate with others at the front (or rear) so everyone maximises their viewing opportunities. Idle chatter and laughter can make animals wary and will spoil the ambience of each site – not just for your group but for other groups in the vicinity. When pointing out an animal or plant to someone keep your voice low or even at a whisper; and similarly, if asking a question of your guide don't shout to attract his or her attention.

Endless Interactions
Seabird colonies are noisy places that attract a host of other animals: finches and mockingbirds looking for food scraps and broken eggs; lava lizards snapping up insects that feed on offal or dead chicks; snakes hunting the lizards; and Galápagos hawks and owls hunting just about everything else.

in niches in lava cliffs, Galápagos hawks scan from prominent boulders, waved albatrosses nest in clearings and many small birds nest in opuntias. And don't forget that human-made structures may also be utilised by some wildlife as perches and nest sites.

Using Calls

Animals communicate with an astonishing variety of vocalisations (or calls) that can help you to locate the callers. Calls that carry a long distance, such as the grunts of mating giant tortoises, can help you decide which direction to begin searching in. Alarm calls often warn of predators on the move; birds usually signal alarm by persistent high-pitched or raucous calls, which are thought to alert others without giving the caller's position away.

Mimicking calls can attract wildlife, especially birds. Pishing (making the 'pish' sound) will entice many small birds; sucking the back of your hand to make a squeaking noise may do likewise. Depending on your virtuosity, numerous trills and whistles can be passably imitated with good results – blue-footed boobies can be fooled into displaying this way. Playing recordings of vocalisations on a portable tape or CD player can be effective for bringing skulkers, such as rails, into the open. But whether playing-back calls or mimicking them, use discretion – they disturb natural behaviour and can provoke stress, territorial displays and occasionally aggression towards people.

Beyond Looking

Most wildlife-watching involves 'collecting' sightings and many wildlifers keep a list of every species they see and where they see it – a practice known as 'listing' or 'ticking' among bird-watchers. Over time, lists reveal which regions and habitats are richest in species and when. Many field guides include a list of species to help you keep track – there's one on p137 of this book.

But as well as keeping a list, look a little closer and spend some time watching even common species; much is still to be learned about all Galápagos wildlife. Try to identify individual animals and distinguish between sexes – easiest in sexually dimorphic animals (where males and females differ in colour, shape or size) such as finches and sea lions. Complex behaviour and interaction goes on constantly, especially in colonial species such as seabirds and pinnipeds, but the most interesting behaviours momentarily cease when animals are alert, such as the first few minutes after you arrive. Wait for them to relax and resume their normal activity. ■

Guides

All tour boats must carry a guide registered with the Galápagos National Park Service (GNPS). These guides, apart from overseeing the safety and comfort of passengers, play a vital role in ensuring national park regulations are obeyed. Guides are qualified as Naturalist I, II or III and all have secondary education and speak some English. You should choose a tour that is accompanied by a Naturalist II or III guide. A Naturalist II guide speaks at least one other language besides English and a Naturalist III guide holds graduate or postgraduate degrees as well as speaking additional languages. A good guide should brief your group before each landing, explaining the salient sights and the day's activities. And don't be afraid to ask questions; in general, Naturalist II or III guides are very well-versed in the natural and human history of the islands, and can be a great asset to your trip. It is possible to visit a few sites on Santa Cruz, Floreana and San Cristóbal without a guide, but hiring one for the day or half-day could make the difference between being safe and getting lost in the rugged terrain if mist closes in.

EQUIPMENT & CLOTHING

Binoculars & Spotting Scopes

Binoculars are the most important piece of equipment you'll ever need for wildlife-watching. They bring everything way up close and help you scan for birds and other animals; they help you locate skulking or cryptic species without scaring them off; and they allow you to watch behaviours from a distance so you don't disturb the participants. There are hundreds of models to choose from, but some basic facts simplify the choice.

Firstly, what do those numbers mean? The first number is the magnification while the second refers to the diameter (in millimetres) of the objective lenses (those furthest from the eye) and indicates their light-gathering efficiency. Thus, 10x40s and 10x50s have the same magnification (times 10; ie an object 100m away will appear 10m away through the binoculars), but the 10x50s admit more light and thus improve the brightness and clarity of the image, particularly in overcast conditions or at dusk. Higher magnifications and, in particular, larger objective lenses both add to the size and weight of binoculars. 'Compacts' (usually 8x20s or 10x25s) fit into a top pocket or under a hat, but performance can be poor in low light, whereas 10x50s can start to feel heavy on long walks, but are clear in all light. Intermediate models, such as 7x35s or 8x40s, are a compromise between the two and are commonly used by bird-watchers and other nature enthusiasts.

It's a good idea to keep cameras in waterproof bags at wet landings, but while travelling in pangas (dinghys) make sure your optical gear is accessible for hard-to-predict photo opportunities.

Binoculars come in many different styles and at prices to suit every budget, but in general the more you pay the better the quality. If wildlife-watching is your passion then you're better off buying a brand with top-quality optics and a casing that is guaranteed water- and dust-proof; with care these binoculars will last you a lifetime.

Spotting scopes are field telescopes that give still higher magnification than binoculars (typically starting at 20x), but usually require a tripod for stability and effective use. A spotting scope would be useful only rarely in the Galápagos.

Clothing

Clothing should be lightweight and fast-drying in the tropical Galápagos climate; muted, natural colours are best. Generally, shorts and light shirts (with collar and long sleeves) will be most comfortable, but trousers provide protection from the sun and insect bites (especially after dark). Full-length cargo pants or the style with zip-off legs that allows you to convert them quickly into shorts are ideal. Sturdy shoes or hiking boots are essential for walking along dusty trails and over lava boulders; wear a pair of durable sports sandals for wet landings and leave them on the beach while you walk the trails. It is essential to wear a wide-brimmed hat to protect against sunburn at all times of year, and good sunglasses to cut down the glare off water and sand. Be prepared for quick changes of weather in the highlands: carry a rainproof and windproof jacket (the sort that can be rolled up and carried in a belt bag) for mist and sudden downpours. ■

Battling the Mist
Binoculars kept in an air-con cabin too long will invariably fog up when you step outside into the humid air. This can be inconvenient and annoying, so before leaving the boat place your binoculars (and cameras or videocams) in the outside air to acclimatise for 10 to 15 minutes, then thoroughly clean the lenses before going ashore.

IDENTIFYING ANIMALS

The distinctive tracks of a female green sea turtle that has hauled ashore to nest at Bahía Gardner, Española.

Field Guides

Field guides are usually pocket-sized books that depict the mammals, birds, flowers etc of a specific area with photos or illustrations. They usually provide identification pointers for each species, and may also include brief natural histories with notes on breeding, behaviour, diet and so on. Guides to animals (especially birds) are usually organised in taxonomic order, a system that shows relationships between species and is more or less consistent between guides; plant guides sometimes rank wildflowers by colour. The merits of illustrated versus photographic guides are debatable; each has its advantages and shortcomings. In general, the value of illustrations depends on the skill of the artist, but many animals are extremely difficult to photograph and photographic field guides are rarely comprehensive. Some people remove the ID plates from guides and have them spiral-bound for ease of use in the field; this will reduce the weight in your pack (especially if you're carrying several guides), but remember that the text often contains the finer points for discriminating similar species.

Biologists are trained to observe and question, and your wildlife-watching experience will be greatly enriched if you do the same. It's also really rewarding to keep a journal of your own observations, adding notes and sketches to what you read in field guides. In practice this is usually difficult in the field because of the excitement of wildlife-watching, but it's a good idea to update any notes as soon as possible after the day's activities as details are easily forgotten. Don't assume that because the book says species X is found here, it must be species X that you're looking at. Birds in particular often wander outside their usual range and many vagrants previously unrecorded in the Galápagos have turned up on migration. If you find something unusual take notes and refer to other books for a positive identification when you get a chance.

Field guides have made an incalculable contribution to the popularity of wildlife-watching. Rarely, though, are they the last word on a subject, and further reading of weightier texts can provide valuable detail not covered in your field guide – see p128 for suggested reading.

Tracks & Signs

Even when you don't see an animal it may leave signs of its presence, such as tracks, droppings, pellets, nests and discarded prey items. There are hundreds of these subtle and not-so-subtle signs and, even if they do not lead you to the culprit, they can enhance your enjoyment of wildlife immeasurably. For example, seabird colonies are littered with egg shells, bones and abandoned nests, even when breeding has finished; old birds' nests, especially those of Darwin's finches, are a feature of opuntias; and 'whitewash' caused by an accumulation of droppings on cliffs can give away a bird's nest or roost – usually a seabird, but sometimes a short-eared owl. ■

> ### Hieroglyphics in the Sand
> An assortment of animal tracks often shows what has been using a sandy beach overnight long after the owners have moved on or taken shelter after sunrise. Tiny indentations made by insects, scorpions and centipedes can be visible, especially in the early morning when the sand is still damp. And it's hard to miss the deep, ladderlike furrows where sea turtles have hauled up to dig a nest in the dunes.

GETTING AROUND

Organised Tours

The seasonal location of most Galápagos wildlife is highly reliable and predictable, making it simple to plan a trip to see what you want at a time that suits you. The vast majority of travellers visit the Galápagos on an organised boat tour and there are several advantages to doing it this way. First, you can pick a vessel and itinerary to suit your interests and budget. Second, it will take some of the hassle out of travel, allowing more time to enjoy the sights. And third, you'll have some guarantee that the boat will provide qualified guides (p28) and will be in reasonable condition.

Of course, you get what you pay for and everyone has a budget and personal tastes to consider. In our experience, small to medium-sized boats carrying 16 to 22 passengers offer the best all-round trip: they are large enough to be comfortable in all but the biggest swell, and the group is small enough to minimise noise and disturbance to wildlife ashore. Several luxurious vessels plying Galápagos waters with anything up to 90 passengers offer a high standard of service and the staff work hard to please everybody, but the sheer number of people queuing up to get ashore and traipsing around the sites may detract from your enjoyment of the experience. This type of cruise is probably not for serious wildlife enthusiasts or photographers, although those who simply desire a holiday-type cruise will still have a memorable experience.

Tour-boat operators design itineraries to visit a variety of sites chosen from the 12 islands open to visitors. No standard itinerary covers them all in a single cruise, and tours vary from day trips to voyages lasting anywhere from a few days to several weeks; most tours, however, last four to seven days. The majority of sailing is done at night so you

wake up and breakfast at anchor; and a well-organised itinerary usually takes in two visitor sites a day, with a walk in the early morning, snorkelling afterwards, lunch as you cruise to another site, then afternoon snorkelling and a walk at the second site.

Doing It Yourself

Independent travel is difficult but not impossible for those with the time to spare, and it offers the serious wildlifer or photographer some advantages, such as being able spend longer in a favourite place. The hardest part is probably getting a flight to or from the Galápagos; tour companies block-book seats and it can be difficult to find an opening as an independent traveller. However, once you overcome this hurdle you could probably pick and choose tours while based in one of the ports, or hitch a lift with a private vessel. Many vessels offer last-minute deals which are considerably cheaper than prebooked cruises. ∎

A small tour boat anchored in the lagoon at Santa Fé. The vast majority of tourists travel between the islands on boats of all shapes and sizes.

Inset: Visitors viewing nesting seabirds from a panga (dinghy) at Tagus Cove, Isabela.

Feeling Just Swell

Hurricanes and even strong winds at sea are unknown in the Galápagos, but a big swell on long crossings can be uncomfortable in a small boat. If you are prone to seasickness you should stick to the more stable lower decks and stern; serious sufferers should ask for a cabin on a lower deck. Motion-sickness tablets are probably the most effective remedy but can cause drowsiness; natural remedies include ginger tablets or wrist bands.

CLOSE ENCOUNTERS

South Plaza is just one of many places where you can see eye-to-eye with large birds such as brown pelicans.

THE Galápagos Islands present a unique opportunity to get up close and personal with wildlife, much of which won't be seen anywhere else in the world and in such close proximity. The vast majority of wildlife you'll encounter will be harmless, intriguing and beautiful. But be aware that this is a natural, tropical ecosystem and there are some invertebrates, such as insects and other arthropods, that can bite or sting. Fortunately, you will rarely see these creatures and by taking some simple precautions you can avoid them almost entirely.

Mosquitoes and blackflies (horseflies) breed in mangroves and near still lagoons; their bites can be irritating but can be avoided by wearing long trousers and long-sleeved shirts where these insects are prevalent, and by slapping a good insect repellent cream on exposed areas of skin. Potentially more serious are the bites of the Galápagos centipede and the sting of scorpions, but these hunters are mainly nocturnal and you have virtually no chance of seeing one on your visit. Just to be on the safe side, don't walk barefoot anywhere except on sandy beaches (the sharp lava fragments on trails will discourage this anyway). The various species of snake are small, retiring and not dangerous to humans; in fact, you will be lucky to see one. The only potentially dangerous large animal is the Galápagos sea lion – some bulls can be aggressive both in and out of the water during the mating season – and you should obey your guide's instructions at all times around these animals. Stingrays are common in sandy bays and have a defensive spine that can inflict a painful sting; however, this sort of mishap is rare and the sting is not life-threatening to adults.

Feeding Wildlife

It is forbidden to feed native wildlife in the Galápagos and with good reason: animals learn very quickly where to get a hand-out and may become pests. Although it is appealing to share a few crumbs with the birds (especially the absurdly tame mockingbirds), be aware that you may be fostering a dependency or affecting an animal's health. Additionally, the artificial concentrations of animals attracted to hand-outs can result in increased aggression between individuals and a greater likelihood that disease will be transmitted. At the very least, you are altering an animal's natural behaviour and it is best avoided whatever way you look at it. Similarly, do not be tempted to put out a container of drinking water to attract birds; the resulting rush can cause injury or even death to birds competing for a drink and dozens of finches have been known to drown in a single bucket of water accidentally left out for a few hours.

Animal Welfare

Although all native wildlife is protected within the Galápagos National Park, feral goats, pigs and donkeys are regularly culled by the Galápagos National Park Service (GNPS) as part of ecosystem management programs. Make no mistake, it is essential to remove these introduced pests (no matter how unsavoury the task) to help maintain or restore the islands' pristine natural environment, and it is done as humanely as possible. However, there is nothing humane in the way fishermen have illegally slaughtered protected species, such as giant tortoises, as a protest against what they see as unfair restrictions on their livelihood. Policing this kind of crime is difficult because of the remoteness of many sites; tourists can help by reporting to the GNPS anything amiss or unusual at a site.

Disturbing Wildlife

At all times when visiting islands (except on parts of Santa Cruz, San Cristóbal and Floreana) you must stick to marked trails and obey your guide's instructions; this is for your own safety as well as to reduce impact on wildlife. The prospects of seriously disturbing animals are slight and usually the worst that will happen is that the subject will move out of sight, which is probably more serious for the viewer than for the animal. Nonetheless, it is important to remember that the presence of people can alter the behaviour of wild animals and you should minimise this wherever possible.

A few pointers should be kept in mind. Never pick up a young animal that looks 'abandoned'. It almost certainly is not and the mother is probably waiting for you to move away before she returns. Some people love to handle small animals, such as lava lizards, but this causes the animal stress (even if it doesn't show it). 'Getting close to nature' is laudable but wild animals are simply never handled; in their experience, being picked up is life-threatening. And don't approach moulting seabirds too closely because they may suffer hypothermia if they are forced to take to the water. Also, note that it is forbidden to use flash photography in the Galápagos; flashes startle wildlife and can cause disorientation in nesting female sea turtles.

The trained naturalist guides working in the Galápagos are invariably excellent. However, if you are uncomfortable with something your guide is doing, don't be afraid to speak up or even report it to your tour company and the GNPS.

Animal Parts & Found Objects

Note that the protection of wildlife in the Galápagos National Park (GNP) also covers parts of dead animals and plants. Thus, found objects such as seashells, bones and skulls, beach-cast coral and even intricate bits of driftwood must never be removed from a site. Guides and other visitors will report you and fines for breaches of GNP regulations are heavy. You almost certainly won't encounter animal skins, live birds, sea-turtle products, sea lion teeth, coral or shells for sale here, but you may do so in mainland Ecuador and some of these may have been collected illegally in the Galápagos. There's no easy answer to the problems posed by hunting or collecting, legal or otherwise, but for visitors, the rule of thumb should be simple: don't buy wildlife products. You are encouraging the unsustainable and often inhumane collecting of wild creatures, and in many cases you may be contravening import regulations in your own country and have them confiscated when you return anyway. ∎

Galápagos sea lions resting on a landing stage at Isla Lobos, San Cristóbal. Bull sea lions may convert a dry landing into a wet one.

BIRD-WATCHING

THERE are some challenges for the hard-core enthusiast, but in general bird-watching in the Galápagos represents quality, not quantity. The relaxed birding pace will allow you time to look closely at seabirds, such as storm-petrels, in (usually) calm seas; marvel over tropical penguins, tame flamingos and flightless cormorants; enjoy other life forms such as sea lions and reptiles; and appreciate the pristine nature of the archipelago. It may even be a relief if you've just arrived shell-shocked from jungle birding in Amazonian Ecuador, but if you simply can't put down your binoculars for five minutes then wet season in the Galápagos brings migratory waders, waterfowl and passerines to pick over for rarities.

How It's Done

All travel between the islands is by boat following an itinerary, which most people sort out in advance through a tour company (p31). The only way to see all the birds (possible in theory) is to take a specialist tour with a bird-watching tour operator (p131) or to charter your own vessel, which is expensive but feasible if you get together with some like-minded people. All boats must carry a licensed GNPS guide, and if you charter a vessel you or your tour company should ensure that the guide is a birding specialist or at least understands the needs of birders. In our experience all GNPS guides can identify the common birds, but even among Naturalist II and Naturalist III guides only a few appear to have any expertise with the finches or seabirds. You'll soon work out your guide's level of interest or expertise, but ask around for a bird expert if hiring one to go into the highlands of Santa Cruz, San Cristóbal or Isabela.

Genovesa supports what is probably the most accessible red-footed booby colony, although this species also nests at Punta Pitt, San Cristóbal.

Top Spots to Go

As with any birding hotspot, the biggest challenge is to see as many species as possible in the time available. Targets for hard-core birders are the 28 endemic species and those subspecies that are potential 'splits' into full species (see the checklist on p137). Like most birding destinations, the majority of resident species in the Galápagos are easy to see in the right place, a few are found at only one or two locations but are common there, and a couple are rare and/or endangered and nigh impossible to see. Only a specialist birding tour or chartered boat will get you past Champion or Gardner-by-Floreana (two small islands to which visitors are not permitted, offshore from Floreana) for

A frigatebird joins common noddies and Audubon's shearwaters at a shoal of fish. Check feeding flocks of seabirds carefully for 'rarities' such as band-rumped storm-petrels.

the Charles mockingbird and visit Bahía Negra (Isabela) for the mangrove finch. Barring mishaps or bad luck, every other breeding or resident species can be seen either by joining a regular tour that visits a few choice sites or under your own steam.

Santa Cruz boasts the highest bird count overall and is the best island on which to get started on the 13 species of finch. The rare lava gull and various large species, such as herons, common noddies, blue-footed boobies and magnificent frigatebirds, are easily seen around Puerto Ayora harbour. Galápagos mockingbirds, large-billed flycatchers, yellow warblers, smooth-billed anis and four common finches should be seen easily at the CDRS (p91). Take a taxi to the highlands and bird the forest at Los Gemelos for woodpecker finches, vermilion flycatchers, large and small tree-finches, Galápagos doves and dark-billed cuckoos. Visit the Giant Tortoise Reserve for Galápagos rails, paint-billed crakes, Galápagos pintails and vegetarian finches; and try Los Tuneles for roosting barn owls.

From there it all happens by boat. Ideally, your cruise should take in Española and you should time your visit to see the waved albatrosses (one of the great seabirds of the world); other specialities here are Galápagos hawks, Nazca boobies, large cactus-finches, Hood mockingbirds and red-billed tropicbirds. Genovesa has red-footed boobies, swallow-tailed gulls and great frigatebirds aplenty, plus the most visible short-eared owls in the Galápagos and the only chance at sharp-beaked ground-finches. Floreana is probably most reliable for greater flamingos and the endemic medium tree-finches; San Cristóbal has the endemic Chatham mockingbirds; and both Isabela and Fernandina offer Galápagos penguins and flightless cormorants (but only Isabela now has mangrove finches). Be vigilant for band-rumped storm-petrels among the storm-petrels, Audubon's shearwaters and dark-rumped petrels at sea. And don't assume all species will be ridiculously tame; the finches in particular can be flighty. On islands where they occur together and possibly interbreed, it is important to get a good look at large, medium and small ground-finches to verify that they are 'pure' (ie nonhybrid) birds.

Field Guides & Checklists

Several species of Darwin's finch are the most difficult birds to identify with confidence in the Galápagos (and you will want to meet this challenge personally, rather than taking someone else's word on ID); storm-petrels are invariably encountered in fast flight at sea and come a close second, but apart from rarities – vagrant seabirds, waders or passerines – an experienced world birder should have no trouble identifying any species here. It is vital therefore that your reference covers the finches and seabirds well, but only two guides do this: *Birds, Mammals and Reptiles of the Galápagos Islands* by A Swash and R Still, and *Wildlife of Galápagos* by J Fitter, D Fitter and D Hosking. Many field guides are out of date or don't cover these groups adequately, and several recent publications treat large, common species in detail but are of little use in identifying others.

Also very valuable are trip reports published by birders who have been to the Galápagos – several basic ones are available for free on the Internet. See p132 for some useful websites. ∎

A large ground-finch at Puerto Egas, Santiago. Fortunately, only a few species of Darwin's finch occur on each island so geographical range is usually a helpful identification pointer.

A juvenile magnificent frigate-bird at Isla Lobos, San Cristóbal. With practice, the two species of frigatebird can usually be told apart in any plumage.

DIVING & SNORKELLING

WITH unique seabirds, mammals and marine life, the Galápagos Islands offer some excellent diving and snorkelling. Don't miss the opportunity to see a penguin 'fly' past underwater or have a juvenile sea lion peer into your goggles; other breathtaking underwater sights include schools of golden rays and hammerhead sharks. Many of the islands have sheltered bays with an array of colourful reef fish and other marine life. At times, cold water, strong currents and/or undertow can add a frisson of excitement for experienced divers, but beginners can enjoy the superb underwater life in complete safety at many sites.

What to Bring

Most cruise boats can provide mask, snorkel and fins for a small hiring fee that usually covers the whole trip, but if you plan to spend a lot of your holiday underwater then consider taking your own gear. If you wear spectacles it may be a good idea to get a mask with glass made up to your prescription or wear contact lenses. The water is coolest from April to August, and both snorkellers and divers are advised to keep warm with a 2mm 'shorty' wetsuit – unless you take a specialised dive tour you'll have to bring this with you. Even in the hotter months it's a good idea to wear some sort of upper-body covering, such as a lightweight polyester swim top or even a T-shirt; the tropical sun is intense and skin burns easily, especially when wet.

Diving

A detailed treatment of diving equipment and sites is beyond the scope of this book, but some basic information is included here. Dive operators in Puerto Ayora (p132) offer certification courses at reasonable prices, regular day trips with wall and shoal diving for beginners and experts around sites close to Santa Cruz, and live-aboard dive cruises on properly equipped vessels to far-flung islands such as Wolf and Darwin. Day-trip destinations include Devil's Crown (Corona del Diablo; Floreana, p84), Rocas Gordon (Santa Cruz, p62), Islas Guy Fawkes (off Santa Cruz), Bartolomé (p71), Cousins Rock (off Bartolomé), North Seymour (p70), Isla Mosquera (near Seymour) and Santa Fé (p68).

Good-quality equipment is available for hire or you can bring the basics and hire the rest there. If you want to try diving with scuba gear, you should have a reasonable level of fitness (although even fit women shouldn't dive if pregnant). Dives vary

Diving with scuba gear will help you discover a wealth of underwater life, such as seahorses, that live too deep to be seen by most snorkellers.

Snorkellers can watch marine iguanas feeding underwater on seaweed at sites such as Punta Espinosa, Fernandina.

considerably according to the degree of experience required, so your logbook is important. Accidents usually result from divers attempting dives beyond their experience.

Snorkelling

You don't need to scuba dive to enjoy the Galápagos' unique marine life – simply by donning mask, snorkel and fins you can experience the myriad inhabitants of a world just a few metres below the surface. Hundreds of species of fish, as well as starfish (sometimes called sea stars), sea urchins, sea turtles and seabirds and other life forms, can be seen in waters less than 10m deep.

Even the timid should try it at least once. The key for beginners is to relax and breathe normally – anticipate a little resistance with the slight change in pressure even just a few inches below the surface. And don't panic when the snorkel fills with water as you submerge; simply blow it clear when you reach the surface. Those who can hold their breath long enough can dive deep and stay deep with power fins and some practice (a technique called free diving), unhampered by cumbersome gear. One more thing: if you can't afford hundreds of dollars for a proper underwater camera, buy one or two plastic disposable cameras (they are often available on board). Although they are rated at a high ISO and thus give grainy shots, sea lions, Galápagos penguins and many fish are so tame that even a rank amateur can get decent underwater holiday snaps.

Strong currents at some snorkelling sites mean it's a good practice to stay with your group rather than striking out on your own.

Top Spots to Go

A typical tour of the Galápagos generally takes in one island per day, and will usually squeeze in at least one underwater foray at that site. Some are better than others, but each site usually has something special about it. Most underwater sites have a similar array of fish, although some are better for, say, white-tipped reef sharks. And unlike the more diverse fishscapes of some other tropical destinations, the Galápagos really crank up the underwater action with tame sea lions, abundant sea turtles and rays, and the world's most unsuspicious and trusting penguins.

Communing with sea lions underwater is high on everybody's agenda, and sea lions will join snorkellers at many sites. But for sheer numbers in calm waters, Isla Lobos (San Cristóbal, p80) and Bahía Barrington (Santa Fé, p68) are probably the picks of the bunch. Sea lions also join in the fun at Tagus Cove (Isabela, p76), but more unusual sights here include Galápagos penguins and golden rays, with a chance of flightless cormorants fishing as well. One of the best sites for watching marine iguanas feeding beneath the waves is Punta Espinosa (Isabela, p76), and in the warm season there are usually lots of green sea turtles here also. If snorkelling is the main reason you came to the Galápagos, then the Devil's Crown off the northern tip of Floreana (p84) is hard to beat for fish and other marine life, including sea lions and sea turtles. This is the most reliable site for hammerhead sharks, although they are mainly seen by divers outside the caldera. Genovesa (p88) is also a top snorkelling spot, with calm, clear water and abundant fish, including many Moorish idols and schools of yellow-tailed surgeonfish. ■

A sea lion pup frolics with snorkellers near Punta Cormorant, Floreana. Close underwater interactions with sea lions are almost guaranteed in the Galápagos.

WHALE- & DOLPHIN-WATCHING

THE rich plankton of Galápagos waters attracts some of the largest animals on earth, the great baleen whales, and vast shoals of fish that support their toothy cousins, the dolphins and blackfish. Although several are known from only one or two records, 25 species of cetacean (the collective term for whales, dolphins and porpoises) have been recorded in the Galápagos, and several others will no doubt occur as whale-watching grows in popularity and identification techniques improve. With much time at sea in a variety of marine conditions – inshore and out on the open waters – cruising the Galápagos is an ideal way to spot a few cetaceans and become familiar with one or two common species.

The telltale falcate (sickle-shaped) dorsal fin of a Bryde's whale in the Canal Bolívar between Isabela and Fernandina. This is one of the most commonly sighted cetaceans in the Galápagos.

How It's Done

Apart from patience and binoculars, cetacean-spotting doesn't demand much in the way of specialised skills or gear. There are no headlands in the Galápagos where cetaceans are regularly spotted, although in theory they could be seen from virtually any coastal lookout. Instead, most viewing takes place from boats, which fortunately provide an excellent platform from which to start looking. Virtually any vessel cruising Galápagos waters will be suitable and close-up views of dolphins riding the boat's bow-wave are not uncommon. Refer to a good whale-watching guide for advice on how to watch these gentle giants without causing them undue disturbance.

There's no particular knack to spotting cetaceans, although practice will hone your skill and calm seas provide the best viewing conditions. Simply scan the water from the highest vantage point with the naked eye, using your binoculars for a close-up view if you see something interesting. The two telltale signs are the characteristic cloud of water vapour that appears when they surface to exhale, called a 'blow' or 'spout', and the arched humps of their dorsum (back) as they surface. Another good indication is a hovering flock of seabirds such as boobies and pelicans, which indicates shoals of fish – irresistible to many dolphins. You could scan fruitlessly for hours so patience will put a natural limit on your efforts, although in Galápagos waters you may well be rewarded with views of other sea creatures, such as manta rays, sunfish and sea turtles.

Identification

With luck your patience will be rewarded with a sighting and then the fun really begins – identifying which species that smooth, most probably blackish, arching glimpse of cetacean dorsum belongs to. The identification of cetaceans at sea (especially whales) can be difficult and usually relies on a combination of features (see the boxed text opposite). Dolphins are usually spotted as they porpoise or breach, but blow is usually the first indication of a whale's presence; note the blow's size, shape (thin or 'bushy') and angle. As the animal's back arches in a dive, note the position of the dorsal fin (the single fin on its back) and its size and shape; some species lack a dorsal fin and this also may be diagnostic. Try to judge the animal's relative size, although this is very difficult at sea, and colour and patterning. Finally, behaviour, such as fluking, porpoising, breaching, logging or spy-hopping, also helps to identify species. Dolphins may travel with pods of other species, such as pilot and baleen whales, and even killer whales (orcas), so keep scanning over pods for anomalous individuals. Remember, only rarely is one characteristic singular enough to identify a cetacean in the field, and you will 'miss' many positive IDs before you get one right. It's all part of the fun.

The field identification of cetaceans is an organic process that feeds the steady improvement in the quality of identification guides. Several good guides are readily available and more are being produced all the time. *Birds, Mammals and Reptiles of the Galápagos Islands* by A Swash and R Still covers all cetacean species known from the archipelago. *Whales, Dolphins and Porpoises* by M Carwardine covers every species in the world with superb illustrations and practical watching tips. *Sea Mammals of the World* by RR Reeves et al is a comprehensive guide to all the world's cetaceans, as well as pinnipeds, and has some stunning photos. See p128 for other recommendations.

Bottlenose dolphins riding a boat's bow-wave near Roca León Dormido (Kicker Rock), San Cristóbal.

Top Spots for Whale- & Dolphin-Watching

Cetaceans – especially dolphins – are encountered on virtually every cruise, although plotting their distribution in anything other than general terms is difficult. One of the best stretches for sightings is the Canal Bolívar, between Fernandina and Isabela, where the movement of water from deeper layers of the sea pushes rich pickings towards the surface for bird and cetacean alike. Bryde's whale is the most common large species encountered, although pods of sperm whale are not unknown and killer whales are often sighted in the channel. Bottlenose dolphins frequently ride bow-waves everywhere in the Galápagos and sometimes large pods are seen fishing; other species sighted regularly include striped and common dolphins. The long cruise up to Genovesa is also reliable for cetacean sightings, especially of deep-sea species such as the mighty sperm whale. Pods of short-finned pilot whales may be encountered virtually anywhere near the central islands. ■

Porpoising & Other Flukish Behaviour

It's worth learning some whale-watchers' jargon to simplify the task of identifying your sightings. Important body parts for identification include the **melon**, the bulbous forehead on many blackfish (large, black members of the dolphin family), and the **notch** (angle) between the **flukes** (tail fins). Dolphins have **beaks** and all cetaceans breathe through either a single or double **blowhole**. Behaviours to watch out for include **fluking** (raising the flukes before a dive), **logging** (lying motionless at the surface) and **spy-hopping** (holding the head clear of the water). Some species slap their flippers on the surface, and **lobtailing** is when an animal lifts its rear end above the surface and slaps the flukes down hard. Many dolphins **porpoise**, leaping clear of the water while travelling at speed, but most spectacular of all is **breaching**, the boisterous display where a cetacean launches itself bodily into the air and splashes down on the surface.

PHOTOGRAPHY

WILDLIFE photography is a highly specialised field, but with some basic attention to technique, and reasonable-quality equipment, you may be surprised at how good your results can be. The enticing tameness of much Galápagos wildlife means even a beginner would be unlucky *not* to take some acceptable shots, but there are many variables to consider. To get the most out of your Galápagos experience you must come prepared.

Equipment

The vast range of equipment on offer makes buying your first camera a daunting task. Most professional wildlife photographers opt for high-quality Canon or Nikon lenses and bodies, mainly because they offer superb optical quality. However, all cameras essentially do the same thing, with varying degrees of complexity and technological features. Most now offer a full range of automatic functions which allow you to 'point and shoot', but make sure your camera allows fully manual operation as well; once you've mastered the basics you'll probably want to experiment.

The most important feature of any camera is the lens, and for wildlife photography, think long and fast. Many animals in the Galápagos are indeed tame but some aren't, and because you must stick to marked trails, subjects such as flowers even a metre away will be out of reach of a basic lens. A 300mm lens is a good starting point, although for bird portraits and close-ups of small species such as lava lizards you'll need something longer. Lenses of 400mm or 600mm focal length are probably out of the price range of many nonprofessionals, although 'slower' lenses (lenses with a relatively low maximum aperture) such as a 400mm f5.6 are reasonably priced and also weigh a lot less. Also consider taking a macro (close-up) lens which allows you to fill the frame with tiny subjects, such as flowers.

Cheaper zooms are generally not as sharp as fixed focal-length lenses (ie lenses that do not zoom), but the difference is only important if you're thinking about publishing your pics. Many makes offer zooms around the 100–300mm range, which, when paired with a short zoom of say 35–70mm, cover most situations for recreational photographers who don't want to carry too much gear. Super zooms provide a comprehensive range of focal lengths in one lens. Canon's 35–350mm and 100–400mm, Nikon's 80–400mm and Sigma's 50–500mm or 170–500mm are worth investigating because they can yield high-quality results in one versatile package. They also offer a lighter alternative to hauling around several lenses, which is welcome given that most wildlife photography in the Galápagos takes place on foot. Canon's image-stabilising lenses (called vibration reduction by Nikon) allow hand-held photography at speeds two to three times slower than normal; they perform extremely well in Galápagos conditions.

Estimate your daily film or memory card requirement then double it; your film or memory card of choice will almost certainly not be available here and you don't want to run out. It's

The Galápagos offer a wealth of natural textures to tempt photographers. Great subjects include the boldly marked marine iguanas at Punta Suárez, Española.

Galápagos wildlife has a reputation for tameness – mockingbirds, in particular, often pose for great shots.

also tempting to go overboard when you see your first sea lions or whatever, when there might be better places to photograph them; in the Islands chapter (p59) we list the best photo opportunities that each island offers. Note that flash photography disturbs wildlife and is forbidden in Galápagos National Park. And be prepared to cope with humidity, salt spray, dust and sand; fit all lenses with a UV filter, and carry the best possible camera-cleaning equipment and use it at the end of each day's shooting.

In the Field

Before you go anywhere, learn how your camera works. Familiarise yourself with its controls and functions by shooting a few rolls at the local zoo or park. Many good wildlife moments happen unexpectedly and pass in seconds; you'll miss them if you're fiddling with dials and settings. For the same reason, leave your camera turned on and pack plenty of batteries – they are scarce and expensive in the Galápagos.

Most cameras have shutter and aperture priority functions. In shutter priority mode, you set the shutter speed and the camera selects the appropriate aperture for a correct exposure; the reverse applies for aperture priority. These two functions are probably the most valuable for wildlife photographers, but you need to know when to use them. Shutter priority is excellent for shooting action: to freeze motion select the highest shutter speed possible in the available light and the camera takes care of the aperture setting. On the other hand, if you're trying to emphasise depth of field in your shot, opt for aperture priority. Large apertures (low f-stops) reduce the depth of field – a useful effect to enhance a portrait shot by throwing a busy background out of focus. If, however, you're shooting a scene where you want everything in focus, such as sea lions sleeping on a long beach, select high aperture (low f-stop).

Look for photo opportunities where wildlife interacts with the human world. This lava heron was snapped at Puerto Ayora, Santa Cruz.

Composition is a major challenge with wildlife because you can't move your subject around; try different vantage points and experiment with a variety of focal lengths. If you're too far away to take a good portrait, try to show an animal in its natural habitat. A 400mm lens might give you a close-up of a booby's face, while a 28mm lens will show the entire colony receding in the background – all from the same position.

Stay still and, above all else when photographing wildlife, be patient. You never know what will appear at a flower next or when a snoozing sea lion will suddenly make a move. You cannot always anticipate an opportunity, but if you're willing to wait you'll almost certainly see something worth shooting. ∎

A fast shutter speed captured water droplets in the wake of this brown pelican as it took off.

HABITATS

The Galápagos Environment
& its Wildlife

OCEANS

A common (brown) noddy silhouetted against the sea at sunset.

THE vast Pacific Ocean isolates and protects the Galápagos archipelago, but paradoxically it has also been the bridge by which the ancestors of many land animals arrived in the islands in the comparatively short span of geological time since they arose from the sea bed (see p18). The highly productive currents that sweep up and down the west coast of South America bathe these volcanic islands in a year-round supply of nutrients: a fine layer of tiny plant and animal plankton that drifts on the sunlit surface and sustains a cavalcade of fish large and small, their predators further up the food chain and some of the largest animals that ever lived – the great whales.

Since much of your trip will be spent cruising between islands, you will invariably encounter many marine life forms that live their entire lives away from land, as well as many that rely on land to some extent for breeding or other phases of their life cycles. Into the first category fall most obviously the many species of pelagic fish. Among them, fast predators such as tuna and jacks hunt in shoals for smaller species, but most predatory of all are the sharks (although oceanic species are rarely seen on casual visits). Flying fish escape predators by flicking their rudderlike tails to become airborne and then gliding for 100m or more on their greatly enlarged pectoral fins. Larger fish species include large 'game' fish, such as marlins, that are occasionally seen jumping; manta rays that can span 7m across the 'wings' and occasionally jump or even somersault above the waves; the strange sunfish, like an enormous disc with fins; and largest and rarest of all, the whale shark, a harmless plankton feeder that can attain 15m or more in length.

Whale sharks, in turn, are dwarfed by the great whales, such as sperm and blue whales. About 25 species of cetacean (the

Previous page: A Galápagos land iguana walking through a dense mat of sea purslane on South Plaza.

Right: The magnificent frigatebird may be encountered far from land, soaring effortlessly on its 2m wingspan or feeding in association with dolphins and tuna and other fish-eating birds.

collective term for whales, dolphins and porpoises) have been recorded in Galápagos waters (see p38), although some are known only from stranded specimens. The most common large species is Bryde's whale, a plankton feeder that attains 15m in length. Killer whales (orcas) are seen with relative frequency, and regularly spotted members of the dolphin family are bottle-nose and common dolphins. Cetaceans are the only mammals that live their entire lives away from land, using the air above only to breathe and display.

Sea turtles and Galápagos sea lions are most common in inshore waters, while birds make up the most frequently seen group of vertebrate animals out to sea. Your boat will almost always be accompanied by delicate, swallow-sized storm-petrels, seabirds that stir up plankton by pattering over the water. Storm-petrels are related to shearwaters, petrels and the great albatrosses, and like them can survive for weeks and even months at sea, returning to land only to breed. These seabirds share one important characteristic: a tube running along the top of their bill that excretes salt absorbed from their environment. The largest species in Galápagos waters, the waved albatross, has long, narrow wings that enable it to take advantage of the air currents set up by the oceanic swell; there are few finer sights at sea than a huge albatross banking effortlessly in the breeze. Seabirds partition marine food resources by feeding in different ways, on different species and at different depths. Thus the pelagic tubenoses feed on or near the surface; the three species of booby dive for fish at different distances from shore; and the frigatebirds snatch flying fish in midflight.

Mammals, such as dolphins and sea lions, and a host of birds, such as boobies, noddies and frigatebirds, commonly gather to prey on the same shoals of fish. These feeding frenzies may involve hundreds of plunge-diving birds and dozens of leaping cetaceans and even marauding sharks in a sea boiling with fish trying to escape. ∎

A white sea urchin and rainbow wrasses. The nutrient-rich waters of the Humboldt Current support a wealth of marine life that in turn feeds the abundant birds and mammals of the Galápagos.

Fish often school in the shade of boats in shallow anchorages, such as at Isla Lobos, San Cristóbal.

COASTS & MANGROVES

A great blue heron hunting among fishing boats anchored in the mangroves at Puerto Ayora, Santa Cruz.

THE shore, or littoral zone, is one of the most dynamic and diverse ecosystems on earth. The immeasurable power of wave action turns cliffs into sand and pounds every living thing in its path, and the ebb and flow of tides alternately submerses animals and plants in salt water then leaves them at the mercy of the sun. It is a vastly productive habitat, picked over by many specialised invertebrates, birds and even reptiles, and exploited opportunistically by many more, including humans.

The thousands of kilometres of coastline surrounding the Galápagos Islands are made up of rocky shores, sandy beaches, sea cliffs, saltwater and brackish lagoons, and mangroves. In common usage, the term 'littoral' refers to the zone between the tides, ie between the usual high- and low-water marks. Technically it also includes the submerged area of the sea floor as deep as light penetrates. But habitat transitions are gradual, and between the littoral and arid (p50) zones there are also sand dunes and their specialised vegetation, plus brackish lagoons that form in shallow depressions.

Rocky shores in the Galápagos are either lava flows still in the process of erosion and hence often brittle and jagged, or the cracked edges of sheer calderas long since submerged by the sea. Either makes a fascinating habitat used by three of the most distinctive Galápagos inhabitants: sea lions, marine iguanas and sally lightfoot crabs. Galápagos sea lions and fur seals feed at sea, the sea lion by day and the fur seal by night, returning to rocky shores to establish territories, mate and give birth, or for rest and social interaction. But marine iguanas rely utterly on this habitat – for the algae growing on the rocks below the waves as sustenance, as a platform on which to thermoregulate and for nesting (on the adjoining beaches). Sally lightfoots, like all crustaceans, have gills and require water to breathe, but they are able to move over land for short spells and can effectively scavenge above and below the tideline. A host of small animals, such as starfish (sometimes called sea stars), molluscs (seashells) and sea urchins live most of their adult lives in the

Opposite page: A green sea turtle swimming in a mangrove-fringed cove. Sea turtles are often seen mating in quiet reaches of such lagoons.

Right: The spectacular sally light- foot crab is a common sight near the tideline on every island.

A brown-phase red-footed booby loafing in a mangrove tree on Genovesa. This is the only booby species in the Galápagos that is light enough to nest in trees.

tidal pools on rock platforms, and myriads of other organisms that never breathe air (too many to even list here; see p127) live their entire lives underwater just a few metres away. Other distinctive and common inhabitants of rocky shores are seabirds and waders, from piebald American oystercatchers chiselling open molluscs to noisy colonies of boobies, storm-petrels and tropicbirds nesting in fractured cliff faces.

Mangroves grow only at the interface between sea and land, a feat that makes them unique among trees and which they achieve with some remarkable adaptations. These plant pioneers colonise muddy shores, their floating seeds taking root and quickly growing in shallow water. Their fleshy leaves excrete salt through special glands, and some species have unique prop roots (pneumatophores), which protrude above the oxygen-starved mud like asparagus spears and enable the plant to breathe. The network of roots in turn traps silt and detritus, eventually stabilising the sediment enough for other, less salt-tolerant plants to take root. And it shelters vulnerable small animals, such as the fry of fish and larvae of crustaceans, until they mature. Thus, mangroves straddle the transition from sea to land, and the four species that grow in the Galápagos tolerate varying degrees of salinity themselves – for example, red mangroves colonise the sea's edge and button mangroves are found closest to land, often abutting stands of terrestrial vegetation. Fiddler crabs, molluscs and small fish forage on the mud among mangrove roots at low tide, in turn attracting predatory birds such as herons and waders.

The sandy beaches of the Galápagos come in several colours, according to the rock from which they were ground or the presence of minerals. They vary from red to green to almost black, as well as some more typical white or golden examples, and come in many textures from pebbles to 'flour' beaches. Beaches are one of the most demanding of habitats, even by littoral standards, with little or no shelter and incessant pounding by the waves. Consequently, they support few life forms and

Ghost crabs are fast-moving hunters that scavenge along the tideline but retreat into burrows when threatened.

Peripatetic sally lightfoot crabs often climb over sunning marine iguanas.

virtually no plants; indeed, most animals found in this tough environment are visitors. Galápagos sea lions are the largest and most obvious, hauling out to doze on the sand; and marine iguanas use beaches as a highway or to lay their eggs. But because they have a high turnover of marine flotsam, beaches also attract many scavengers, such as ghost and hermit crabs, lava gulls, and plovers and sanderlings that snatch morsels from incoming waves.

The dunes behind beaches mark the often blurred transition from the littoral to the Galápagos' arid zone, and many land animals, such as lava lizards and mockingbirds, forage in both. Dunes support a characteristic suite of vegetation, such as saltbush and succulent sea purslane (also known as carpetweed), which can resist the salt spray and help bind the sand. One large animal, the green sea turtle, relies totally on dunes for reproduction, hauling up the sand to lay its eggs above the highwater mark. Where a shoreline has shifted or uplifted, or where the process of vegetation succession has cut off backwaters, shallow, brackish lagoons may form. These are highly productive areas for many birds, such as waders, Galápagos pintails and greater flamingos, all of which feed on tiny animals and microscopic plants that thrive in the warm, sunlit waters. ∎

The shallow but sheltered mangrove lagoons at Punta Espinosa, Fernandina, are excellent places to see rays, fish and sea turtles.

Battle of the Sea Cucumbers

Sea cucumbers, known locally as *pepinos*, are sausage-shaped marine animals related to starfish and sea urchins. *Pepinos* ingest sand from which they extract food particles and thus turn over vast quantities of sediment on the sea bottom; they play a vital role in maintaining the health of marine ecosystems. Some Asian cultures regard these useful animals as a delicacy for their supposed aphrodisiac qualities and harvesting sea cucumbers is a lucrative international business whose tentacles have stretched even to the Galápagos. Despite complete protection in Galápagos waters, international demand encouraged an illegal harvest for many years, especially around Isabela and Fernandina. Galápagos National Park Service (GNPS) patrols confiscated millions of dried *pepinos*, and in 1997 a park guard was shot by poachers. Under extreme pressure from the fishing lobby, the GNPS implemented a policy of sustainable harvest for the local fishing industry, with tight limits. Illegal fishing remains a problem despite improved patrolling efforts. *Pepino* numbers now appear to be significantly reduced, largely due to the illegal activities. Meanwhile conflict continues around trying to find an alternative livelihood for the *pepino* harvesters.

ARID ZONE

Lava cactus at Punta Espinosa, Fernandina. The short, cylindrical stalks grow to 60cm in height and clumps may measure 2m or more across.

COVERING much of the islands' surface is a rather forbidding landscape of poor soils and volcanic spoils, punctuated by bristling cacti that tower above the surrounding vegetation. Daytime temperatures soar to 30°C (86°F) and beyond, and the little rain that falls during the wet season quickly drains away or evaporates in the intense sun and prevailing winds. Life in this arid zone is a challenge for every living thing, yet this is the most diverse vegetation zone in the archipelago, rich in endemic plants and home to virtually all of the land birds and reptiles. The arid zone covers extensive lowland areas on all the main islands, and on small islands it's usually the only terrestrial habitat, starting virtually at the high-water mark.

Palo santo (sometimes called torchwood) is one of the most widespread woody plants in the Galápagos and covers whole hillsides at some sites, where its smooth silvery bark gives the landscape a bleached look. Arid-zone plants have evolved different strategies to conserve moisture or repel solar radiation, or both. *Palo santos*, for example, are deciduous – they drop their leaves during the dry season to conserve moisture, quickly sprouting a mantle of green when the rains arrive. And, like most arid-zone plants, they have wide root systems that suck up rainfall from the shallow soils. Other plants, such as *chala* (Galápagos croton), cut down evaporation with narrow leaves that minimise the surface area exposed to wind and sunlight.

However, the cacti take water conservation to extremes and are among the most successful and distinctive arid-zone plants. The spines have actually evolved from leaves and double as protection for the spongy pads, which evolved from branches and can hold moisture. The endemic lava cactus is a pioneer species that takes root in the cracks in barren lava flows. Largest and most outstanding are the famous prickly pears of the genus *Opuntia*, which in the Galápagos have evolved into six endemic species and many varieties (see Missing the Point, p53).

Opposite page: A sparse covering of grey matplants helps to stabilise the dusty slopes of Bartolomé.

Right: Opuntias dominate the arid zone on some islands, even growing down to near the splash zone on Rábida's cliffs.

Animals have much higher energy requirements than plants and must balance the need to find sustenance with moisture conservation. But, paradoxically, reptile diversity peaks in this zone, and lava lizards and iguanas are among the most obvious inhabitants. Reptiles have a low metabolic rate, relying on ambient temperature to raise their body temperature to a 'working' level and surviving on minimal nutrition or food of low nutritional value (as long as it is available in adequate supply). After spending the night inactive they quickly attain optimal body temperature for feeding after sunrise, and many individuals and species can coexist in a given area because each needs comparatively little to survive. Giant tortoises and land iguanas acquire their moisture requirements from succulent plants; and snakes and lava lizards do so from the juicy invertebrates that abound in this habitat.

Birds are also abundant in the arid zone: mixed flocks of ground-finches forage for seeds; cactus-finches probe opuntia blossoms for nectar; and mockingbirds and Galápagos doves supplement plant food with insects. Most birds – especially seed-eaters – will drink daily if water is available, but fresh water is a luxury for most of the year and they can satisfy their needs from moist plant matter. Insect-eaters and carnivores, such as flycatchers and Galápagos hawks, obtain their moisture needs from their prey. Where the arid zone borders the coast on some islands, it has even been appropriated by nesting colonies of garrulous seabirds that look quite at home among the cacti. But overheating is a real danger for their eggs and chicks, and parent birds spend much time standing over their nests in the blazing sun, cooling off by fluttering their naked throat patches.

Of course, many of the larger inhabitants of this habitat couldn't survive without smaller animals to sustain them, and the arid zone supports many species of invertebrate. Painted locusts and various butterflies are among the more colourful examples, but dragonflies breed in ephemeral pools during the rains and hundreds of other species usually remain hidden from visitors. Invertebrate life cycles are invariably packed into a few

A candelabra cactus in flower at Puerto Baquerizo Moreno, San Cristóbal. This statuesque species has edible fruits and grows to a height of 8m.

Sea purslane is a succulent that grows in dense mats and turns rust-red or orange during garúa season (June to November).

Missing the Point

Opuntias (also known as prickly pears) have coevolved with many arid-zone animals and play an integral role in their life cycles. Cactus-finches have beaks adapted for probing cactus flowers and depend on these plants for food and nest sites. Land iguanas and giant tortoises eat the juicy pads, both apparently oblivious to the tough protective spines, and male land iguanas fight to protect their 'patch' of opuntias. On islands where these reptiles occur, prickly pears tend to grow into trees with tall stems that put the edible parts out of reach; conversely, where tortoises and land iguanas are absent, opuntias grow as a 'bush', with the pads at ground level. Opuntias are pollinated mainly by native carpenter bees, but on Genovesa, where the bees are absent, Galápagos doves take over the role of pollinator and the cacti have evolved soft, pliable spines that allow the doves access to the flowers. Coincidentally, iguanas and tortoises are also absent from Genovesa.

short weeks of plenty during the rains, their eggs lying dormant during the long dry season and hatching when conditions are suitable. Some species, such as predatory scorpions and centipedes, are active only at night when ambient temperatures are lower, and shelter during the day under rocks or in burrows.

The arid zone stretches from near sea level to an altitude of about 200m, although its upper limit can range from 500m on northern slopes to as low as 100m on southern slopes. In general, as one travels higher up a mountainside the soil gets deeper and the rainfall higher, and the 'transition zone' marks the change from the arid zone to the moist highlands (p54). But it's only a gradual change: typical arid-zone plants get fewer, epiphytes become more prevalent and the undergrowth gets denser as you climb. The transition zone is restricted to Santa Cruz, Isabela, Floreana and San Cristóbal, but much of the natural vegetation has been irrevocably altered by agriculture and cattle-grazing. Native trees, such as *pega pega, guayabillo* and *matazarno,* have largely been supplanted by banana, coffee and citrus trees to feed burgeoning population centres and the tourist trade. This zone features many land birds, especially finches and those that can survive in close proximity to people, and giant tortoises, although none is restricted to this zone and most are best seen elsewhere. ■

Palo santo *forest on the slopes of Volcán Darwin, Isabela. The fragrant bark is covered with pale lichen, which from a distance gives this tree its distinctive 'bleached' look.*

Cactus-finches are restricted to the arid zone, and are common among the tall opuntias on Rábida.

HIGHLANDS

The yellow flowers of muyuyo trees add a splash of colour to the arid and transitional zones.

MOIST air that evaporates off the waters surrounding the Galápagos is blown against the high peaks of large islands, such as Santa Cruz and San Cristóbal, where it cools down and falls as rain. By midmorning the peaks are often hidden by cloud that creates a cool world of shifting mists and frequent showers, cloaked in myriad greens that present an extraordinary contrast with the hot, dry lowlands. During the wet season the rainfall can be substantial, but time of year scarcely makes a difference and the fine mist known as the *garúa* blows almost constantly across the hills during the dry.

The peaks have eroded into rich, volcanic soil supporting dense vegetation communities that soak up precipitation like a vast green sponge. Owing to prevailing southeasterly winds, this 'moist' zone extends lower on the south slopes than the north. It can be further divided into three distinct but slightly overlapping zones: the humid 'cloud forest' zone with a high, closed canopy dominated by trees such as *guayabillo, pega pega* and scalesia (tree daisies); the miconia zone, composed almost entirely of an endemic shrub, *Miconia robinsoniana*; and the *pampa,* or fern-sedge, zone.

The scalesias are an endemic genus of the daisy family (see p56) and the tree scalesia is so dominant on Santa Cruz and several other islands that the area where it grows is described as the scalesia zone. (The other 19 species of scalesia are found throughout the islands in a variety of habitats and don't grow so tall.) On large islands the scalesia forest starts after the transition zone, as low as 200m on southern slopes but as high as 700m in places with a northerly aspect. It is a sodden, misty world of dense greenery, the tree daisies towering up to 15m high and festooned with trailing beard moss and vines. Every available surface of trunks and branches is covered in lichens or labours under the weight of miniature gardens of epiphytes, such as dripping mosses, ferns, orchids and bromeliads. Detritus adds to cushions of moss and leaves on the forest floor, which

Opposite page: Scalesia forest towers above a hiker at Los Gemelos in the Santa Cruz highlands. These 'tree daisies' grow to a height of 15m and support waterlogged clumps of epiphytes.

Right: A dragonfly in the Santa Cruz highlands. Dragonflies and damselflies spend their larval stage in fresh water, and only eight species manage to survive in the Galápagos.

Tree ferns at Los Gemelos in the Santa Cruz highlands. In damp, sheltered hollows these endemic ferns may reach 6m in height.

Miconia growing at El Junco Lagoon in the highlands of San Cristóbal. Miconia leaves turn reddish during dry periods.

serves as a rich bed for the proliferation of dense shrubs, flowering herbs, club mosses, liverworts, and more species of fern, bromeliad and orchid.

This is one of the most exciting wildlife-watching zones in the islands and well worth visiting (see p62 for more information). With the possible exception of the small Fernandina rice rat, no native mammals or birds live exclusively in this zone, although some birds, such as the dazzling vermilion flycatcher, are more commonly found here. Small birds are abundant, and among a variety of Darwin's finch there are large and small tree-finches, warbler finches and the amazing woodpecker finch (p119). Galápagos rails and paint-billed crakes forage in the dense, soggy undergrowth and dark-billed cuckoos hunt for insects in the canopy. The only reptiles that survive in this cool climate are giant tortoises, whose great size enables them to cope with low temperatures: greater size decreases the ratio of body weight to surface area, and thus reduces heat loss, enabling the tortoises to survive here and take advantage of the ample herbage as food. Like the tree daisies, the tortoises also attained gigantism for the simple reason that they could (ie there was no competition to prevent them from becoming the dominant herbivores in the Galápagos). Flowering herbs and shrubs attract an assortment of insects, such as the large-tailed skipper (a butterfly), and the larvae of wood-boring beetles feast on rotting trunks and logs. The highlands are also rich in land snails of the endemic genus *Balimulus*.

Where Daisies Grow into Trees

'Typical' trees have comparatively large seeds unable to survive immersion in salt water for long (apart from notable exceptions such as mangroves) and few species have been able to reach the Galápagos by natural means. But in any case it would have been too late, for the niche normally occupied by trees was already filled by a flower! The endemic tree daisy *Scalesia pedunculata* belongs to the widespread plant family that includes dandelions and thistles, adaptable plants whose tiny seeds are easily spread by the wind. Seeds of the ancestral tree daisy were among the first to take root when the barren Galápagos Islands first emerged from the sea. Finding no competition, they proliferated and adapted to fill many available niches, including that normally occupied by forest trees. The 19 other endemic species of scalesia are scattered throughout the Galápagos in a variety of habitats, and many other endemic plants belong to this family.

Some researchers divide these altitudinal zones still further, and recognise a 'brown' or zanthoxylum zone growing between the scalesia and miconia zones. This habitat is dominated by cat's claw, also known as wait-a-minute bush, which is typically draped in epiphytic mosses that give it an untidy, deep brown look. Little of this habitat now remains on Santa Cruz.

Miconia robinsoniana is a distinctive shrub that grows in stands so dense it has given its name to another vegetation zone that once covered entire hillsides above the scalesia zone. Usually no more than 2m high, it has broad, brownish leaves and a pink flower spike, and grows only on the very wet, high southern slopes of Santa Cruz and San Cristóbal, usually starting at about 400m above sea level. Most of the miconia zone has now gone, cleared for agriculture or choked out by introduced weeds, and is now best seen at Media Luna on Santa Cruz (p62). It's a treeless, quiet world with many species of moisture-loving grasses, liverworts and ferns, especially bracken. The main vertebrates in this cool zone are birds, including woodpecker, tree- and ground-finches, flycatchers, Galápagos rails and endangered dark-rumped petrels, which breed in burrows underneath the miconia.

A giant tortoise in the grassy highlands of Santa Cruz.

The *pampa*, or fern-sedge, zone grows at the highest and therefore wettest elevations, ie above 500m, and occurs only on the largest islands. It is essentially an upland moor, composed of low grasses, sedges and ferns, with an understorey of colourful lichens. The largest plant is the Galápagos tree fern, which can tower 3m above surrounding vegetation in sheltered nooks. Several native orchids are endemic to this zone and sphagnum moss grows in waterlogged depressions. Few visitors see this habitat and the only permanent large inhabitants are probably Galápagos rails skulking in the undergrowth. ■

Highland landscape of miconia and bracken at El Junco Lagoon, San Cristóbal.

ISLANDS

The Best Wildlife-Watching
Destinations in the Galápagos Islands

PUERTO AYORA (SANTA CRUZ)

Wildlife at All Hours in Sleepy Port

Lava herons hunt crabs and other small animals at Puerto Ayora's busy harbour, apparently oblivious to the goings-on around them.

A flowering tree adds a splash of colour to Puerto Ayora's streets.

Previous page: Tourists being ferried back to their boat as the sun sets behind Santiago and Bartolomé's Pinnacle Rock.

THE picturesque little port that handles the bulk of the Galápagos' tourist trade is expanding rapidly into the hinterland of Santa Cruz, but many widespread animal species are still easily seen around town. Indeed, many apparently live oblivious to humans, while others actively exploit the inevitable by-products of human activity, using artificial structures for their homes and scavenging food around hotels and dwellings. The negative side of human impact should not be downplayed, of course, and expanding settlement inevitably means the disruption of more habitat to make way for buildings, roads and services. Perhaps more seriously, animals and plants that commonly associate with humans, such as rats, dogs and other vermin, can pose a direct and serious threat to native wildlife.

If you arrive by bus from Baltra, you will alight next to Puerto Ayora harbour, where **lava herons** hunt the **sally lightfoot crabs** crawling across the pilings. This is actually one of the best places to see the world's rarest gull, the **lava gull**, which like many of its kind loiters near moored boats watching for scraps thrown overboard. If you arrive by boat, look for **Galápagos sea lions** surfacing in Bahía Academy, **Elliot's storm-petrels** flitting among the vessels riding at anchor and **magnificent frigatebirds** floating overhead. The western edge of the harbour is an eroded caldera on which nest **blue-footed boobies** and **common noddies**, particularly on the cactus-studded cliffs of Laguna Las Ninfas.

Established in 1964, the Charles Darwin Research Station (CDRS; p91) makes a great introduction to birds of the arid zone and gives you a chance to get up close and personal with captive **giant tortoises**. Most tours include a visit to the station, but you are also free to go there independently. There's a plan of the station near the entrance and it's worth dropping in to Van Straelen Hall, where illustrated display panels explain in simple terms the physical and living environment of the Galápagos, and introduce conservation and research themes; there's a short video presentation and station personnel give talks from time to time.

At the CDRS you'll see the incubators where tortoise eggs are hatched and pens where youngsters of various subspecies are raised until they are old enough to be released into the wild on their respective islands. The trail follows raised walkways and informative display boards to the corrals containing adult tortoises, including some giant males, an Española 'saddleback' and Lonesome George, the last survivor of the distinct Pinta subspecies. The large cement water dishes in the tortoise corrals attract **Darwin's finches**, **yellow warblers**, **large-billed flycatchers** and Galápagos mockingbirds. These artificial watering points are great places to get acquainted with at least four species of finch (**large**, **medium** and **small ground-finches**, and **cactus-finches**) and nut out the subtleties of their identification. You'll also see **Galápagos land iguanas** in breeding pens from where endangered populations are restocked.

Smooth-billed anis are common along the entrance road to the CDRS and the station is a good place to look for skulking **dark-**

billed cuckoos. Marine iguanas sometimes attempt to nest in the scoria footpaths along the entrance road, and if you walk along here at night with a torch you could see **yellow-crowned night herons** hunting rodents and large invertebrates. The night herons, plus **brown pelicans** and **lava herons**, also hunt under the tall streetlights down by the docks, where native **bats** can sometimes be seen catching insects around the lights. You'd have to be lucky (or confident) to work out which species they are. Other night sights include **geckos** – both native and introduced species – hunting insects on walls around town.

The mangroves that fringe Bahía Academy support nests of **great blue herons** and **brown pelicans**, both of which are easily seen resting on docks and even on the walls of waterfront hotels. **Yellow warblers** and other birds, including occasional **vegetarian finches**, are common in well-treed hotel grounds, where big, grey **Galápagos lava lizards** scuttle among rockeries. **Marine iguanas** can be seen right next to the main street along the waterfront, especially where fishing boats land their catches; and **cattle**, **great** and **snowy egrets** fly overhead as they head for their mangrove roosts at dusks.

Take a water taxi to the landing stage at Angermeyer Point and follow the walking trail to Playa de los Alemanes. On the way you'll pass several mud flats where you'll see various **herons** and **shorebirds**, such as **black-necked stilts**, **whimbrels** and **semipalmated plovers**. These brackish lagoons are good hang-outs for migrants, such as **phalaropes** and the occasional **belted kingfisher**.

Playa Tortuga makes a good day trip along a paved path through arid-zone vegetation; you don't need a guide but it's a popular spot so get there early if you want some peace and quiet. The pavement ends at a fine white-sand beach where **lava gulls** scavenge, and **sanderlings** and **semipalmated plovers** pick morsels along the tideline. **Green sea turtles** nest among the low dunes decked with distinctive Galápagos club-leaf shrubs and beach morning-glory vines. A rocky promontory divides the beach from a wide, mangrove-fringed lagoon with nesting **brown pelicans** and **great blue herons**. The water isn't too clear, but green sea turtles visit the quiet waters to mate and **greater flamingos** are sometime visitors. Migratory waders, including occasional **short-billed dowitchers**, probe the sand in shallow tidal pools behind the dunes. There's a short loop trail around the rugged point that passes nesting **blue-footed boobies**, **lava herons** on the hunt, some tall opuntias and tons of **marine iguanas** that nest in the coarse sand. ∎

Facilities Puerto Ayora has restaurants, bars, Internet cafés, bookshops, souvenir shops, dive operators and most services. Dry landing at Puerto Ayora.

Accommodation Enough to suit all tastes and budgets is available in Puerto Ayora.

Contact Cámara de Turismo (Tourist Information Office; ☎ 05-526206; www.galapagostour.org; Avenida Charles Darwin), TAME (☎ 05-2526527; www.tame.com.ec; Avenida Charles Darwin).

Wildlife rhythms Migratory wader numbers peak from December to March; green sea turtles nest at Playa Tortuga from December to June.

Photo opportunities Great blue herons, marine iguanas, blue-footed boobies, migratory shorebirds.

SANTA CRUZ (INDEFATIGABLE ISLAND)

Galápagos Central

Wildlife Highlights
Intact stands of all Galápagos vegetation zones and their representative wildlife, including dense scalesia forest and miconia. The archipelago's most accessible population of giant tortoises. Bird list of some 85 species includes nine Darwin's finches, rarities such as Galápagos rails and breeding dark-rumped petrels, and many vagrants. Highlands feature giant tortoises, vermilion flycatchers, woodpecker finches, Galápagos rails and short-eared owls. Tranquil lagoons at Caleta Tortuga Negra support golden and spotted eagle rays, herons and waders; Playa Bachas supports greater flamingos and waders. Cerro Dragón for flamingos, Galápagos pintails, waders and a small population of rehabilitated Galápagos land iguanas.

LYING centrally in the archipelago, Santa Cruz is a large, high island on which volcanic activity has long since ceased, although there are some interesting geological remnants. The wetter southeast side faces into the trade winds and has the archipelago's largest human population; Puerto Ayora (p60) is the administrative centre for the Galápagos National Park Service (GNPS) and Charles Darwin Research Station (CDRS; p91). With a long history of settlement and agriculture, much of the natural landscape has been irrevocably altered by introduced plants and animals, but Santa Cruz still offers easy access to all vegetation zones, including good stands of highland forest, and has the highest bird tally of any island.

Most travellers land at scantly vegetated Baltra, also known as South Seymour, where you might see one of the **Galápagos land iguanas** that have been reintroduced near the airport. You're bound to see a few **frigatebirds** overhead and **small ground-finches** poking around the terminal. To get to Santa Cruz from Baltra you must cross the Canal de Itabaca, where you should see **sally lightfoot crabs** and **marine iguanas** on the lava rocks, and **brown pelicans**, **blue-footed boobies**, **common noddies** and **lava gulls** along the cliffs. Look around the bus stop where you wait for your lift to Puerto Ayora for small and **medium ground-finches**, and **small tree-finches**. The road to Puerto Ayora passes through all the vegetation zones, from the arid zone with *palo santo* trees and many cacti to the lush highlands, then back down to sea level again at Bahía Academy.

Despite its large size, a juvenile brown pelican is light enough to be supported by a mangrove tree in Puerto Ayora harbour.

Giant Tortoises & Rare Birds in the Mist

The road passes between Los Gemelos (Twins), two large craters formed by the collapse of empty magma chambers. This is the most accessible patch of endemic scalesia forest in the Galápagos, an eerie world of shifting mists and frequent rain with great birding. The loop trail around the western crater is best, and passes through dripping, mossy trees festooned with epiphytic beard moss, orchids and ferns, and back via the crater lip. **Small ground-finches** and **warbler finches** can only be described as abundant, and **vermilion flycatchers**, **small tree-finches** and **yellow warblers** are also

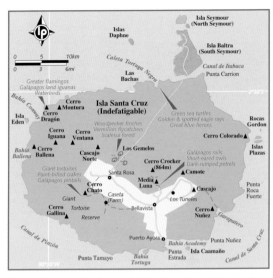

common. **Galápagos doves** fly about at the craters' edges and in the crater floors, and the elusive **dark-billed cuckoo** is also here. But the real prizes are the **vegetarian** and **woodpecker finches**, both of which may be found after careful searching. **Large-billed flycatchers** hawk from the forest edge and **short-eared owls** are in the area, although you may have to scan long and hard with binoculars among the crevices of the crater cliffs. Botanists will revel in the array of endemic tree and maidenhair ferns, bromeliads, club mosses and Darwin bush.

A good stand of miconia is accessible north of Bellavista on the slopes of Media Luna and Santa Cruz' highest point, 864m Cerro Crocker. Take a taxi uphill to the park boundary – turn left past the plaza and follow the only road past some farms to where the road ends; it's an easy downhill walk back to Bellavista. The miconia zone starts just inside the fence, where you'll see signs of the quinine tree control program and, in the distance, dense stands of this pest species where it hasn't yet been killed off. It's generally quiet apart from a few **finches**, such as **small ground-finches** and **woodpecker finches**, although this is a good site for **short-eared owls**. The real prize up here is the elusive **Galápagos rail**, which is common although far more often heard than seen. **Dark-rumped petrels** nest in burrows among the miconia, but you'll have to wait till dusk at the right time of year to see them returning. Along the road back to Bellavista, **yellow warblers**, small ground-finches and **small tree-finches** are common; **smooth-billed anis** and **cattle egrets** lurk in the fields and **paint-billed crakes** are sometimes seen in brakes of rank grass by the road. Some lava tubes (natural tunnels formed by lava flow) on a private farm east of Bellavista – Los Tuneles – can be a good site for roosting **barn owls**, and the surrounding vegetation here and back along the road to the town offers another chance at seeing **tree-finches** and **vegetarian finches**.

Location Central island and main tourist hub.

Facilities Snacks and drinks available at Giant Tortoise Reserve, Los Tuneles and Bellavista; see also Puerto Ayora (p60). Wet landing at Las Bachas, dry landing at Cerro Dragón; no landing at Caleta Tortuga Negra.

Accommodation Available in Puerto Ayora.

Contacts GNPS, TAME and Cámara de Turismo in Puerto Ayora.

Wildlife rhythms Sightings of sea-turtle matings peak in January; most nesting takes place in the warmer months, peaking in February. Female giant tortoises descend to arid zone to nest in dry season. Dark-rumped petrels breed in miconia zone year-round.

Photo opportunities Giant tortoises, vermilion flycatchers, woodpecker finches, golden and spotted eagle rays, great blue herons, greater flamingos, Galápagos mockingbirds.

Sunrise over Bahía Academy in Puerto Ayora.

Santa Cruz supports the largest population of **giant tortoises** (about 3000) after Isabela, and the Giant Tortoise Reserve near Santa Rosa is an ideal place to see them in the wild. Pools near the start of the trail down to 'the reserve' often have **Galápagos pintails**, and this is as good a place as any to wait for **Galápagos rails**. The trail leads down through secondary forest heaving with **smooth-billed anis**, **Galápagos** and **vermilion flycatchers**, and **Darwin's finches**, including **woodpecker finches**, **large ground-finches** and **large tree-finches**; **paint-billed crakes** are also sometimes seen along the way. Giant tortoises could be encountered almost anywhere on the trail and even among the **whimbrels** and domestic animals in fields adjoining the dirt road down from Santa Rosa. More are present in the dry season, when the females have returned from egg-laying in the lowlands, but the huge males make an impressive sight and can be seen at any time of year. Overgrown pools at the end of the trail near Cerro Chato hold **moorhens (gall-inules)** and more Galápagos pintails, but they can be hard to see among the vegetation.

Tranquil Lagoons & the Hill of Dragons

Caleta Tortuga Negra (Black Turtle Cove) stands out as one of Santa Cruz' best coastal sites, but this network of peaceful, mangrove-fringed lagoons on the north coast is accessible only by *panga* (dinghy). Your *pangero* will steer the dinghy through the narrow rocky entrance, where **common noddies** and **blue-footed boobies** perch on the rocks, into the sheltered waterways beyond. **Green sea turtles** are common and in season can often be seen in mating pairs or clusters. Young **white-tipped reef sharks** can sometimes be seen in the clearer, seaward lagoons, but are rather shy and fast-moving. However, this is one of the best sites to see schools of **spotted eagle** and **golden rays**, winging silently through the water. Red, white and black mangroves at the edge of the lagoons are draped with the scattered nests of **great blue herons** and **brown pelicans**. **Greater flamingos** are occasional visitors and low tide sees **lava herons** hunting at the water's edge. **Waders** such as **whimbrels** join **Galápagos mockingbirds** and **yellow warblers** and the occasional dozing **Galápagos sea lion** on the mud among the mangrove roots.

Named after some barges wrecked offshore during WWII, Las Bachas is a wet landing on a white-sand beach backed by

Return of the Iguana

The Galápagos land iguana was once common on several islands, but introduced species have threatened its survival. Eggs are dug up by feral pigs and dogs, feral livestock tramples nests, and cats, dogs and pigs prey on the young. Land iguanas disappeared from Baltra during WWII, and were all but wiped out on Santa Cruz by dogs by 1976, when the Galápagos National Park Service (GNPS) and Charles Darwin Research Station (CDRS) rescued the last 60 remaining in the wild. About 40 of the survivors were transferred to Venecia, a small island off the north coast near Cerro Dragón, with soil moved from their natural habitat to establish an artificial nesting site. This technique proved so successful that juveniles hatched on Venecia are repatriated to Cerro Dragón every second year. The remaining adults, held at the CDRS, were released back into the wild. Cerro Dragón was developed as a visitor site in 1995 and the wild population there has also started to breed again, although predation by cats remains a constant threat.

a saltwater lagoon. **Great blue herons** often stalk the lagoon among **Galápagos pintails** and **black-necked stilts**, or feed among the rock pools at low tide. **Brown pelicans** and **blue-footed boobies** plunge-dive close inshore, and **waders** such as **sanderlings**, **wandering tattlers** and **semipalmated plovers** trot along the beach. Nesting **green sea turtles** haul up the sand to nest in the dunes during the warmer months and **marine iguanas** bask on the rocks between the beaches. The snorkelling is OK but the water can be turbid; early starters might get a lucky glimpse of baby **black-tipped reef sharks** before they get spooked by swimmers.

A small population of **Galápagos land iguanas** has been reintroduced to Cerro Dragón and pest control is ongoing, although you may still hear and see signs of feral donkeys. **Marine iguanas** and **sally lightfoot crabs** await visitors at the rocky landing, and **Galápagos pintails** frequent a small pool nearby. The trail winds past dense mats of sea purslane to a shallow lagoon which can be excellent for waterbirds. **Greater flamingos** are reasonably reliable here, and among **lava herons**, **black-necked stilts** and more Galápagos pintails could be **waders**, such as **grey plovers**, **least sandpipers**, **wandering tattlers** and **whimbrels**, and **Franklin's** and **laughing gulls** sitting out the high tide. It's an easy walk to a low hill where the first land iguanas are encountered – usually within safe reach of their burrows. The mixed scrub is made up of *palo santo* and mesquite trees, spiny bush, Galápagos croton and Galápagos cotton punctuated with opuntias and candelabra cacti. Animal encounters will probably include **large-billed flycatchers**, **Galápagos mockingbirds**, and **small** and **medium ground-finches**. Large **painted locusts** hop across the trail, and the webs of **spiders** adorn the vegetation; watch for **common cactus-finches** among the opuntias. ■

Watching Tips
All of the highland sites can be visited without a guide and it would be hard to get lost anywhere except in the Giant Tortoise Reserve. But if you want to seek out the bird specialities, ask around Puerto Ayora for a guide who knows birds and make sure they know what you want to see. Arrange for a taxi to pick you up early (preferably about 6am), and take wet-weather gear, water and stout walking shoes or gumboots.

A great blue heron hunting at sunset before flying to roost.

SOUTH PLAZA (PLAZA SUR)

Good Things in a Small Package

> ### Wildlife Highlights
> One of the best islands for Galápagos land iguanas can also boast a very high density of Galápagos sea lions and great seabird-watching. Land iguanas abundant among opuntias and marine iguanas abundant along rocky shores, with sally lightfoot crabs and occasional iguana hybrids in between. Swallow-tailed gulls, common noddies, red-billed tropicbirds, blue-footed and Nazca boobies, and Audubon's shearwaters nest along sea cliffs. Three species of Darwin's finch, including hard-to-miss cactus-finches, and rarities such as kelp gull and peregrine falcon have turned up as well as regular migratory waders.

Tall opuntias and extensive mats of sea purslane make the tilted surface of South Plaza ideal habitat for land iguanas.

THE two Islas Plazas (Norte and Sur, meaning North and South, respectively) are uplifted slabs of sea floor, rather than volcanic islands like nearby Santa Cruz, separated from each other by a channel less than 1km wide. Only South Plaza is open to visitors, but boats usually anchor closer to the steep, fractured cliffs of North Plaza, which swarm with **common noddies** and **swallow-tailed gulls**. Flocks of **Audubon's shearwaters** wheel about, **red-billed tropicbirds** show off their aerobatic skills, and both **blue-footed** and **Nazca boobies** wing down the channel. Both islands rise from a flat northern edge and tilt gently up to steep 25m cliffs on their southern side. And although South Plaza is barely 1km long and 100m wide it supports an amazing variety of wildlife.

It's a short *panga* ride across to the southern island, where a bull **Galápagos sea lion** often dominates the GNPS dock; many other sea lions will be seen on both shores of the channel, hauled up on the rocks asleep, lazing in the shallows or porpoising through deeper water. Ever-watchful **lava gulls** loiter for a feeding opportunity and **marine iguanas** compete with **sally lightfoot crabs** for space on the rocks. South Plaza is small enough for a marine iguana to walk right across, and a meeting with a **Galápagos land iguana** is inevitable for marine iguana and human alike; indeed, hybrid iguanas are known to occur. South Plaza's land iguanas are one of the smallest subspecies, and stake out territories under the shade of the impressive opuntias that stud the sloping hillside.

On the short track up the gentle incline to the breezy southern cliffs the sprawling littoral-zone vegetation, with extensive carpets of succulent sea purslane, changes to dense stands of saltbush and leatherleaf and back to an open boulderscape pierced by large opuntias. The number of prickly pears across

the island explains why so many **Galápagos land iguanas** survive here; it's estimated some 250 to 300 adult iguanas live on South Plaza. **Yellow warblers** are common but the only finches are **medium** and **small ground-finches**, and **cactus-finches**; this is a good place to watch the cactus-finches in particular. **Lava herons** hunt the colourful **sally lightfoot crabs** along the shore, and **great blue herons** and **cattle egrets** are also recorded occasionally, the latter picking off **lava lizards** and large insects among the **Galápagos sea lions**.

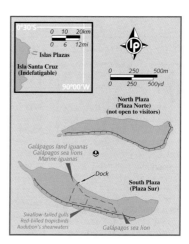

High Action along Clifftops

The 1km loop trail heads east along the edge of the wind-buffeted southern cliffs, where cracks in the brittle lava provide nesting sites for **seabirds**. This is an ideal place to watch and photograph **red-billed tropicbirds** in flight as they display and return to their nests in the crevices. Nesting **swallow-tailed gulls** are abundant and unsuspicious, and take advantage of sites right at the cliff's edge; **common noddies, blue-footed boobies** and the occasional **Nazca boobies** (inset) nest or roost on ledges below; and **brown pelicans** loaf just above the reach of the waves. **Audubon's shearwaters** chase each other in fast flight at eye level and **magnificent frigatebirds** hover on thermals high above the cliffs.

Use the cliffs' vantage points to scan the offing (the expanse of visible sea) for **Galápagos** and **Elliot's storm-petrels**, flocks of wintering **red-necked phalaropes** (in calm seas) and **cetaceans** such as **bottlenose dolphins**. **Peregrine falcons** have been sighted here on migration and one could easily be missed as it sits still on a high ledge. **Short-eared owls** are the only resident raptor but they also use nooks in the cliff for nesting and roosting.

The trail turns downhill again at a colony of bachelor **Galápagos sea lions** – old, spent bulls living out the rest of their days free of the stress of territorial fighting. But there's no such insouciance back at the channel, where bulls battle for mating rights with the dozens of sea lion cows that haul out along here. South Plaza is estimated to support a peak population of about 1000 Galápagos sea lions and the bulls make snorkelling highly inadvisable. Along the shore look for migratory **waders**, such as **sanderlings, whimbrels, wandering tattlers, ruddy turnstones** and **semipalmated plovers**. There's also usually a pair of **American oystercatchers** somewhere along the shore, and **kelp gulls**, stragglers from southern latitudes, have been recorded here. Snorkelling is possible around boats at anchor or along the shore of North Plaza; with luck you'll be joined by juvenile sea lions, and the fish-watching is quite good, although the current can be strong. ■

Location A few hundred metres off the east coast of Santa Cruz; 30km northeast of Puerto Ayora.

Facilities None; dry landing. Landing not permitted on North Plaza.

Wildlife rhythms Female land iguanas nest on the eastern side of the island during the wet season. Peregrine falcons are most likely to be seen between November and March.

Photo opportunities Galápagos land iguanas, red-billed tropicbirds, Galápagos sea lions, swallow-tailed gulls.

> **Watching Tips**
> Hybrid iguanas are generally dark in colour like marine iguanas, but can be easily told apart by their pale, evenly spaced 'zebra stripes'.

SANTA FÉ (BARRINGTON ISLAND)

Playful Sea Lions in Idyllic Bay

Wildlife Highlights
Many playful juvenile Galápagos sea lions a treat in turquoise lagoon with reef fish, spotted eagle rays and green sea turtles. Endemic land animals include Santa Fé land iguanas and Santa Fé rice rats among forests of giant opuntias. One of the best sites for Galápagos hawks. Galápagos doves, mockingbirds and lava lizards common. Other land birds include cactus-finches. Seabirds such as blue-footed and Nazca boobies, brown pelicans and red-billed tropicbirds. Great diving outside harbour with hammerheads a major attraction.

Santa Fé's opuntias are among the tallest in the archipelago and have a massive, straight trunk.

MUCH of Santa Fé's surface is an eroded, faulted plateau that formed when basaltic lavas oozing out of submarine fissures some four million years ago were forced above the sea by volcanic uplifts. Today it is covered with arid-zone vegetation, such as giant opuntias, and its age and isolation have allowed several endemic animals to evolve, including species of **land iguana**, **rice rat** and **gecko**. Black rats never invaded Santa Fé, but introduced goats caused widespread habitat destruction and browsed heavily on Heller's scalesia, a distinctive subspecies of daisy tree that grows along the coast. The goats were eliminated in the 1960s, and with the resulting reversal of habitat destruction the scalesia has recovered and the rice rat also appears to have benefited.

There's only one visitor site, tranquil Bahía Barrington, where the turquoise water makes an idyllic anchorage behind a chain of islets that forms a natural breakwater. **Green sea turtles** and **spotted eagle rays** cruise over the sandy bottom; **brown pelicans** and **blue-footed boobies** rest on the rocks; **Nazca boobies** wing along the coastline; and **magnificent frigatebirds** soar overhead. But the most obvious sight to greet visitors is the abundance of **Galápagos sea lions**. There are two sea lion beaches at the head of the bay, with up to 50 on one and 80 on the other. Pups are left on the beach while their mothers are away feeding, but juveniles cavort beside *pangas* ferrying visitors ashore, doze in untidy piles on the fine white sand and lava boulders, and readily join snorkellers in the lee of the breakwater. Other underwater encounters in the bay could include **marine iguanas** feeding among the jumble of submerged lava boulders, **sea urchins**, fish such as **yellow-tailed surgeonfish**, **Panama sergeant majors**,

king angelfish and **parrotfish**, **stingrays** and occasional **white-tipped reef sharks**. The best snorkelling is in the lee of Isolte Black, the large islet that forms the seaward end of the breakwater. Santa Fé is also a popular dive spot, with clear water and mild currents on the seaward side of the breakwater; **garden** and **moray eels**, and white-tipped reef sharks and **hammerheads** are among the attractions.

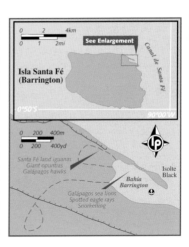

Land of the Giants

A long trail (1.5km each way) follows a dry watercourse up a high escarpment to the southwest; it's a hot walk, and you'll probably see **Santa Fé land iguanas** along the way, but most people do it for the great views. The second, more popular, walk is an 800m track that climbs to a giant opuntia forest growing above coastal cliffs then loops through arid-zone vegetation back to the bay. This trail begins on Bahía Barrington's fine white-sand beach, where **Galápagos lava lizards** dart between the saltbushes and leatherleafs or display from wooden trail-markers. **Galápagos mockingbirds** are common, picking their way among sunburnt legs and sleeping **Galápagos sea lions**. Boulder steps take you up through

Galápagos croton bushes and *palo santo* trees – where **Galápagos doves**, **yellow warblers** (inset) and several species of **Darwin's finch** feed and nest – and pretty soon you're dwarfed by Santa Fé's unique subspecies of giant cactus. The reddish trunks can measure 2.5m in girth and the crown may be 10m above the ground, and the Santa Fé land iguanas think they're special too: males stake out and fiercely contest territories under productive trees. In fact, the interaction between cactus and lizard may have forced the plants to grow tall, straight trunks so the iguanas couldn't eat all the succulent pads. **Cactus-finches** also depend on the prickly pears for food and nest sites, and Galápagos mockingbirds poke opportunistically among the pads.

The endemic **Santa Fé rice rat** is still common in the arid zone and if you are lucky enough to spot one they are usually unsuspicious and trusting. Heller's scalesias grow along the edge of the cliffs, and you can look out to sea for **red-billed tropicbirds** and **Nazca boobies**, and along the track for **warbler finches**, **small ground-finches** and **large-billed flycatchers**. **Marine iguanas** have been known to climb up from the rocky shore below, and **Galápagos racers** hunt **lava lizards** and **painted locusts** among the boulders on the hillside. Santa Fé has a healthy population of **Galápagos hawks** and these could be seen anywhere: riding an updraft next to the cliffs, perched on the park monument or on one of the large cactus trees on the point at Isolte Black. ∎

Location 20km southeast of Puerto Ayora.
Facilities None; wet landing.
Wildlife rhythms Most sea lion pups born in *garúa* season; rice rats breed in the wet season.
Photo opportunities Santa Fé land iguanas, Galápagos sea lions, Galápagos hawks, giant opuntias, Santa Fé rice rats.

Watching Tips
Rice rats are primarily nocturnal, but rustlings among the leaf litter might give away their presence, especially in the early morning or late afternoon.

NORTH SEYMOUR

Good for Starters

Wildlife Highlights

Breeding seabirds a speciality, with good numbers of blue-footed boobies, swallow-tailed gulls, common noddies and both magnificent and great frigatebirds. Both Galápagos pinnipeds present; Galápagos sea lions common but fur seals less frequently seen on casual visits. A few Galápagos land iguanas live near trails and marine iguanas are common along the shoreline. Other seabirds include smaller numbers of lava gulls, Nazca boobies, Audubon's shearwaters and red-billed tropicbirds, and two species of storm-petrel usually close inshore. Several species of endemic plant.

Location Small island 40km north of Puerto Ayora.
Facilities None; dry landing.
Wildlife rhythms Blue-footed boobies breed mainly in *garúa* season; frigatebirds and swallow-tailed gulls breed year-round.
Photo opportunities Blue-footed boobies, swallow-tailed gulls, great and magnificent frigatebirds, Galápagos land iguanas.

Watching Tips

On islands where predatory giant tortoises and land iguanas are naturally absent, such as North Seymour, endemic opuntias grow as a low 'bush'.

THE discovery of marine fossils on this plateau surrounded by low cliffs indicates that North Seymour is an uplifted lava flow, like several other small islands near Santa Cruz. Seymour's flat profile makes for easy walking and offers an accessible introduction to the archipelago's unique animals and plants.

After negotiating the **Galápagos sea lions** draped over the landing dock you'll probably come face-to-face with the two endemic gulls, **swallow-tailed gulls** and **lava gulls**; the former breeds in good numbers along the cliffs where **common noddies** also nest. Heading inland, the trail loops through mixed vegetation that includes several endemic plants, such as the characteristic dwarf *palo santo* that often grows in association with an endemic opuntia. **Blue-footed boobies** and a few **Nazca boobies** nest in open areas among clumps of *muyuyo* and saltbush; the main concentrations of blue-foots are near the start of the trail and at the far end near the frigatebird colony. **Magnificent frigatebirds** (inset) make up most of the colony, especially in the middle, but **great frigatebirds** occupy saltbushes towards the edges. **Galápagos land iguanas** can be seen along the way, particularly as they emerge from their burrows after sunrise. These lizards are not native to North Seymour, but were presci-

ently brought here from nearby Baltra (also known as South Seymour) by scientists in the 1930s. The Baltra population subsequently died out and the North Seymour iguanas have since formed the nucleus of animals that were recently reintroduced there. **Lava lizards** hunt among the rocks and mats of sea purslane, and in turn are hunted by **striped Galápagos snakes**. Small birds include **yellow warblers, Darwin's finches** and **Galápagos mockingbirds**.

Heading back along the shore, some impressive waves breaking against the tumbled boulder wall provide a noisy backdrop and fine salt mist to wildlife activity. More **blue-footed boobies** rest on the sand, and **Galápagos sea lions** haul out to sleep, flicking away **sally lightfoot crabs** that wander too close; watch for young sea lions and, occasionally, **bottlenose dolphins** surfing the fine breakers. North Seymour's very dark **marine iguanas** nest on this beach and **waders**, such as resident **American oystercatchers** and migratory **sanderlings** and **turnstones**, join **brown pelicans** and **great blue herons** sitting out the high tide on the rocks.

Cliffside nooks are occupied by nesting **red-billed tropicbirds** and **Audubon's shearwaters**; and out in the channel, watch for the two common **storm-petrels, Galápagos** and **Elliot's**. **Galápagos fur seals** haul out to sleep in the lee of the cliffs, but they are not readily seen from the clifftops and a *panga* ride is usually necessary to see this pinniped. ∎

BARTOLOMÉ

Geological Showcase

PINNACLE Rock – the remains of an eroded tuff cone – leans into Bartolomé's northern bay and provides one of the most recognisable landmarks in the Galápagos Islands. The island is really two barren volcanic cinder cones, connected by a green isthmus bordered by golden sand beaches. Scan the surrounding waters as you approach the island for **bottlenose dolphins**, flocks of **red-necked phalaropes** in season, **storm-petrels** and **dark-rumped petrels**.

Galápagos penguins live at the foot of the rock, to which you can swim from shore or take a dinghy, and can often be seen swimming near its base or in the bay itself. There's good snorkelling among the jumbled boulders at the foot of the rock. Many visitors have underwater encounters with the penguins, but there are also inquisitive **Galápagos sea lions** plus an assortment of marine life, such as **parrotfish**, **Mexican hogfish**, **yellow-tailed surgeonfish**, **Panama sergeant majors**, **whitetail damselfish**, **green sea** and **pencil-spined urchins** and **chocolate-chip sea stars**; **white-tipped reef sharks** are sometimes seen but are wary of swimmers.

It's a five-minute walk to the southern bay through a dense stand of mangroves where you'll probably see **yellow warblers**, **small ground-finches** and Galápagos doves; Galápagos lava lizards scuttle along the hot sand and **painted locusts** jump across the path. This beach is often devoid of people but is patrolled by **ghost crabs** scuttling into their burrows, and resident **American oystercatchers** and migratory **semipalmated plovers**.

Galápagos hawks drift overhead and tracks of **green sea turtles** mark the dunes behind the beach. **Brown pelicans** and **blue-footed boobies** plunge after fish in the shallows and **Galápagos penguins** occasionally surface.

It's an easy hour's climb to the summit of the 114m spatter cone via a dock draped with **Galápagos sea lions**. Little moves on these slopes apart from **Galápagos lava lizards** hunting the few invertebrates that can eke out an existence among the pioneering matplants and spurge that punctuate the barren volcanic ash. Hardy lava cacti grow on the slopes, a few opuntias survive on high bluffs and scalesias struggle up the north face. The main reason to climb the cone is to get up close and personal with the volcanic phenomena packed into this small area. Lava tubes, some whole and some partly collapsed like gutters, festoon the slopes, particularly on the eastern side. From the summit – where you'll get a panoramic view of the archipelago – you can also see reddish spatter cones, *hornitos* ('little ovens'; also called driblet cones) and, in the right light or at the right tide, a large submerged crater in the sea below on the north side. ■

Wildlife Highlights

Small but scenic with spectacular examples of volcanism on slopes of extinct spatter cone. Narrow isthmus supports Galápagos penguins and sea lions on rocky shores; brown pelicans and blue-footed boobies on cliffs; waders and nesting green sea turtles on beaches; and Galápagos lava lizards, Galápagos doves and yellow warblers all over. Good visibility for snorkelling with Galápagos penguins and cavorting sea lions in the northern bay.

Location In Bahía Sullivan, east of Santiago; 115km northwest of Puerto Ayora.

Facilities Dry landing and marked trail to summit; wet landing on beach.

Wildlife rhythms Green sea turtles nest January through March; Galápagos penguins resident; phalaropes visit surrounding seas November through March.

Photo opportunities Volcanic phenomena, American oystercatchers, ghost crabs, marine life.

Watching Tips

Snorkelling is not permitted off the southern beach, but black-tipped reef sharks and rays are sometimes seen in shallow water from shore.

SANTIAGO (JAMES ISLAND OR ISLA SAN SALVADOR)

Tranquil Former Haunt of Pirates

Wildlife Highlights

Puerto Egas, the archipelago's best site for Galápagos fur seals, which cohabit rock platforms with Galápagos sea lions, large marine iguanas and yellow-crowned night herons. Productive rock pools picked over by lava herons, American oystercatchers and other waders. Arid-zone vegetation supports Darwin's finches, Galápagos hawks and abundant Galápagos doves. Blue-footed boobies and occasional Galápagos penguins roost on rocky point with good fish-watching in clear water. Playa Espumilla's lagoon excellent for waders; many Galápagos sea lions and nesting green sea turtles at Buccaneer Cove.

THE official name of this island, Isla San Salvador, is used less often than the old Spanish name (Santiago), or the English name (James). Rising to a height of over 900m, Santiago is large enough for an endemic subspecies of **giant tortoise** to have evolved, although you are unlikely to see it at the visitor sites. This was also where Darwin famously complained about the number of land iguana burrows, but, sadly, land iguanas have vanished thanks to predation by feral pigs and rats. Feral donkeys and some 100,000 goats have also had a serious impact on this largely arid environment and GNPS eradication programs were commenced in the 1970s. Curiously, Santiago's endemic **rice rat**, not seen since 1906 and presumed extinct, was rediscovered in 1997 and thus appears to have persisted alongside the introduced black rat.

Buccaneer Cove was an important site for 17th- and 18th-century sailors to reprovision with water, tortoises and firewood. There are plenty of **Galápagos sea lions** on the beach here, but most vessels visit Playa Espumilla to the south, where the golden sand features nesting **green sea turtles**, **ghost crabs** and **waders**. Dense mangroves surround a network of brackish lagoons behind the beach that were once an important site for **greater flamingos**, although the birds deserted the site after the disastrous 1983 El Niño and are now only irregular visitors. However, the lagoons are excellent for **Galápagos pintails** and waders, such as **black-necked stilts** and **whimbrels**. The short trail is good for **Darwin's finches**, and **vermilion** and **large-billed flycatchers**.

Puerto Egas (South James Bay) was another buccaneers' supply base and the remains of abandoned 20th-century salt-mining operations are scattered over the site; these days **Galápagos hawks** use the derelict buildings as a vantage point. This attractive site is dominated by Pan de Azúcar (Sugarloaf Hill) and the black-sand beach is bounded by low tuff cliffs sculpted by wind and sea. **Galápagos sea lions** cool off under the roof of a natural arch at the western end of the beach, where **marine iguanas** and **sally lightfoot crabs** roam the rocks. The webs of **zigzag spiders** span the botanically interesting trail that leads through *muyuyo*, lantana, spiny bush and morning-glory, and is dotted with occasional opuntias. **Insects** are abundant during wet season, with butterflies such as **fritillaries** and **Galápagos sulphurs**, **dragonflies**, **carpenter bees** and **painted locusts**. Galápagos doves are common and other land birds include **Galápagos mockingbirds**, **smooth-billed anis**, **small ground-finches** and **large-billed flycatchers**.

A collapsed lava tube at Puerto Egas forms a sheltered grotto and playground for Galápagos sea lions (pictured) and fur seals.

Fur-Seals' Hideaway

Heading west, the trail leads to a series of collapsed lava tubes that open to the sea and have formed grottos with clear water and natural arches. This is the best – and

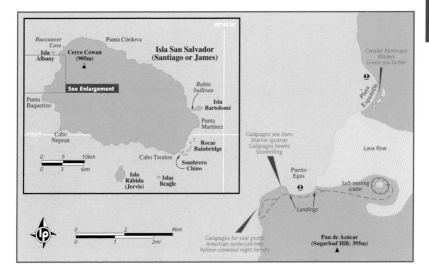

most picturesque – site anywhere to see **Galápagos fur seals**, which rest here under shady overhangs or loll about in the turquoise pools. Both species of pinniped are here – there's no reason why **Galápagos sea lions** shouldn't enjoy the grottos as well – but the smaller fur seals clamber higher up the cliffs. **Yellow-crowned night herons** while away the daylight hours in the shade of overhangs, and **lava herons** stalk **sally lightfoots** in the rock pools.

It is possible to walk along the rock platforms and tidal pools on the way back to the beach. **American oystercatchers** are resident on the point and the rich pickings attract other **waders**, such as **ruddy turnstones**, **semipalmated plovers**, **least sandpipers**, **wandering tattlers** and **whimbrels**. Heading east, the trail ascends through *palo santo* trees to a crater, formerly mined for salt but now used occasionally by **greater flamingos**.

There's good snorkelling in clear water off the point, where you might be watched by **brown pelicans** and **blue-footed boobies** or the occasional **Galápagos penguin** loafing on the rocks. Underwater sights include **Mexican hogfish**, **king angelfish**, **wrasses** and **triggerfish**; thousands of **salenias** gather to mate and spawn at times, attracting **white-tipped reef sharks** and other predators.

Bahía Sullivan on the east coast marks the edge of a vast lava flow that spewed out as recently as 1900. There's a tiny landing beach with **Galápagos penguins**, but few plants have colonised the lava's barren surface and only **lava lizards** hunt over the twisted loops of pahoehoe lava among pioneering *mollugo* (a low herb) and lava cactus. Like adjacent Bartolomé, Bahía Sullivan is mainly of interest for its evidence of volcanism. Obsidian, dense volcanic glass, has formed at the edges of fissures where the lava has split, showing layers of older flows underneath; other sights to look out for include *hornitos* and the moulds of trees vaporised by the heat. ∎

Location Central in archipelago; 85km northwest of Puerto Ayora.

Facilities None; wet landings at all sites.

Wildlife rhythms Best wader-watching at Playa Espumilla November to March; green sea turtles nest mainly during wet months.

Photo opportunities Galápagos fur seals, waders, marine iguanas, yellow-crowned night herons.

Watching Tips
Tidal pools at Puerto Egas support diverse invertebrate life including starfish (sometimes called sea stars), sea anemones and seashells such as tuns clinging to rocks at low tide.

RÁBIDA (JERVIS ISLAND)

The Red Island

> **Wildlife Highlights**
> Greater flamingos share a brackish lagoon with bachelor Galápagos sea lions, nesting brown pelicans, Galápagos pintails, black-necked stilts and various heron species. Both pinnipeds are present: Galápagos sea lions easily seen on sandy Playa Rojo and fur seals doze on shady rock platforms. Waders, ghost crabs and Galápagos mockingbirds forage along the beach and land birds include Galápagos hawks, abundant Galápagos doves and nine species of Darwin's finch. Good snorkelling with schools of reef fish, Galápagos penguins, blue-footed boobies and brown pelicans.

RÁBIDA'S most striking feature is a high bluff on the north coast, which glows a startling rust red when the sun is low in the sky and contrasts with the green fringe of straggling opuntias along the summit. The towering cinder cliffs have eroded into long, sandy beaches of the same warm shade and make a striking backdrop to the **brown pelicans**, and **blue-footed** and **Nazca boobies** loafing on the sheer walls. More cactus clumps dot the hillsides leading up to the red island's 367m eroded volcanic peak. Rábida has never supported giant tortoises or land iguanas, and the opuntias here have evolved into a 'bushy' form with soft spines and abundant fruit. Feral goats have been eradicated and much of Rábida's vegetation and wildlife remains more or less pristine.

Galápagos sea lions, **green sea turtles** and **Galápagos and Elliot's storm-petrels** investigate boats riding at anchor, and sea lions also huddle along the aptly named Playa Rojo (Red Beach), although this strip of sand is seemingly too narrow to entice the sea turtles into nesting. **Waders** such as **American oystercatchers, semipalmated plovers, ruddy turnstones** and **sanderlings** work the tideline along the beach. Human landing parties galvanise **Galápagos mockingbirds** into investigating the visitors almost as soon as they arrive; **ghost crabs**, on the other hand, scuttle back into their burrows when approached too closely.

Playa Rojo is backed by dense saltbush and clumps of spiny bush, which hide a brackish, mangrove-fringed lagoon and the island's main attraction, a small flock of **greater flamingos**. Walking west along the beach, there's a short trail to the edge of the lagoon. Flamingos used to breed here, but bachelor **Galápagos sea lions** wallowing in the muddied water eventually forced them to abandon their nesting efforts; indeed, the sea lions have been known to use flamingos' nests as pillows! There are usually at least a few of the pink birds about, but look under the overhanging branches of mangroves at the back of the lagoon for **Galápagos pintails** and other waterbirds, such as **whimbrels, black-necked stilts** and **great blue** and **lava herons**. **Brown pelicans** nest on these trees, and on the bushes between the lagoon and the shore.

Guano from nesting boobies dots the high cliffs on Rábida's north coast.

Birds Above & Below the Waterline

A 750m trail east of the lagoon climbs past some tall mangroves, from which **Galápagos hawks** sometimes keep watch, and up onto a headland sparsely vegetated with lichen-encrusted *palo santos*, Galápagos croton and leatherleaf. **Galápagos doves** (opposite) break from cover along the way and other small birds include **yellow warblers, large-billed flycatchers** and **Galápagos mockingbirds**. This is the

place to look for some of Rábida's nine species of **Darwin's
finch**; the trail is particularly
good for **cactus-finches** among
the stands of opuntia, and
other common species include
warbler finches, and **small,
medium** and **large ground-
finches**. Several vantage points
look across the strait to Santiago before the path loops
around the point above more
red cliffs, bristling with prickly
pears that grow right down to
the splash zone, just above the
farthest reach of the waves.
Magnificent frigatebirds ride
the updrafts over the headland

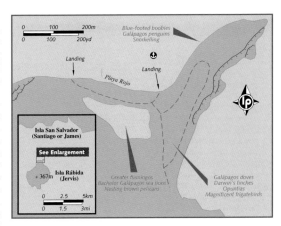

and **brown pelicans** and **blue-footed boobies** hurtle down the
breeze as they scour the sea for prey.

A *panga* ride along the base of the headland cliffs is the best
way to see the **Galápagos fur seals** that flop out under sheltered
overhangs during the day. And below the waves, both sides of
the promontory offer good snorkelling in clear water despite the
occasional buffeting from the surge. Schools of **reef fish** include
**king angelfish, yellow-tailed surgeonfish, triggerfish, concen-
tric puffers** and **Mexican hogfish**; and huge congregations of
spawning **salenias** attract predators such as **white-tipped reef
sharks**. Galápagos penguins, blue-footed boobies and brown
pelicans roost on rocky ledges just above high-water mark and
will usually allow a close approach for snorkellers armed with
waterproof cameras. Rábida is a good site to watch these birds
fishing, the penguins barrelling along underwater after small fry
and the pelicans and boobies plunge-diving close inshore – even
among parties of snorkellers. Of course, no underwater outing
would be complete without an inquisitive **Galápagos sea lion**
and Playa Rojo's pinnipeds usually oblige.

Bottlenose dolphins are commonly encountered around
Rábida and could even be seen from shore from the headland;
short-finned pilot whales are also known from these waters,
and **Audubon's shearwaters, waved albatrosses, swallow-
tailed gulls** and **lava gulls** are all sighted regularly at sea. ∎

Location 5km south of Santiago, 60km northwest of
Puerto Ayora.
Facilities None; wet landings at
Playa Rojo.
Wildlife rhythms Brown
pelicans nest mainly in *garúa*
season.
Photo opportunities Greater
flamingos, Galápagos sea lions,
ghost crabs, opuntias.

Watching Tips
Watch from the head-
land for large schools of
the endemic yellow-tailed
mullet, which swim in lines
just below the surface.

ISABELA (ALBEMARLE ISLAND)

The Restless Giant

> **Wildlife Highlights**
> Numerous visitor sites offer great scenery and diverse wildlife-watching. Volcanic massifs support five endemic subspecies of giant tortoise, plus Galápagos land iguanas and nine species of Darwin's finch. Giant tortoises roam the slopes of Volcán Alcedo in good numbers, and females descend to nest at Bahía Urvina, where Galápagos land iguanas are resident. Tagus Cove offers seabird highlights such as Galápagos penguins and flightless cormorants, plus snorkelling with Galápagos sea lions. Secluded mangrove lagoons at Bahía Elizabeth and unusual brackish pools in a volcanic wasteland at Punta Moreno. Canal Bolívar supports large marine iguanas and many seabirds, and offers a good chance of seeing Bryde's and killer whales.

THE vast lava flows of six major and numerous smaller volcanoes have uplifted and joined over millions of years to form what is now the island of Isabela. By far the largest landmass in the Galápagos, Isabela measures more than 130km from north to south and 70km at its widest point. And it is still active: 1646m Volcán Wolf erupted in 1982 and 1689m Volcán Cerro Azul as recently as 1998, and uplifts continue to reshape the coastline. Isabela has several unique animals, including the world's only surviving population of **mangrove finch**, and **giant tortoises** that have been isolated long enough on their respective volcanoes to evolve into distinct subspecies.

Puerto Villamil isn't on the itinerary of most cruise boats, but it is the starting point to ascend Sierra Negra, the only active volcano in the Galápagos that could be climbed by visitors at the time of writing. Quinta Playa, a brackish lagoon west of town, is one of the best **greater flamingo** sites in the Galápagos and has resident **Galápagos pintails**, **black-necked stilts** and **moorhens (gallinules)**. The muddy shores of this and other pools nearby attract regular migratory visitors, such as **ruddy turnstones**, **semipalmated plovers** and **whimbrels**, and rarities that might include **blue-winged teals**. A **giant tortoise** breeding station north of town run by the CDRS raises and repatriates the two subspecies of giant tortoise that live on Isabela's southern volcanoes.

The waters of the Canal Bolívar between Isabela and Fernandina are one of the best stretches in which to see cetaceans (whales and dolphins) in the Galápagos. Be on the lookout during daylight hours wherever you travel between the islands. **Bryde's whale** is the most common large species encountered, but the channel is also a reasonably reliable area for **killer whales (orcas)**, and it would be an unlucky trip that didn't see a pod or two of **bottlenose dolphins**. Large fish regularly sighted include **manta rays** and the bizarre **sunfish**, which is like an enormous disc with fins; and the southern end of the channel is one of the few places in the Galápagos where giant **whale sharks** have been seen. Birds commonly encountered at sea include the usual **Audubon's shearwaters**, **Galápagos** and **Elliot's storm-petrels**, **common noddies**, **blue-footed boobies** and, in season, **waved albatrosses**. **Dark-rumped petrels** are uncommon but always present in small numbers and rarities could include **sooty terns** and **black storm-petrels**.

Steam rises from volcanic fumaroles on Sierra Negra. Isabela and Fernandina are the two most volcanically active islands in the archipelago.

Sheltered Lagoons & Strange Vibrations

The west coast of Isabela is rich in wildlife, particularly where the massifs of Volcán Alcedo and the Sierra Negra join to form a sheltered kink in the coastline. Punta Moreno is reached through mangrove-fringed lagoons with breeding **brown pelicans**, and **flightless cormorants** and **American oystercatchers**

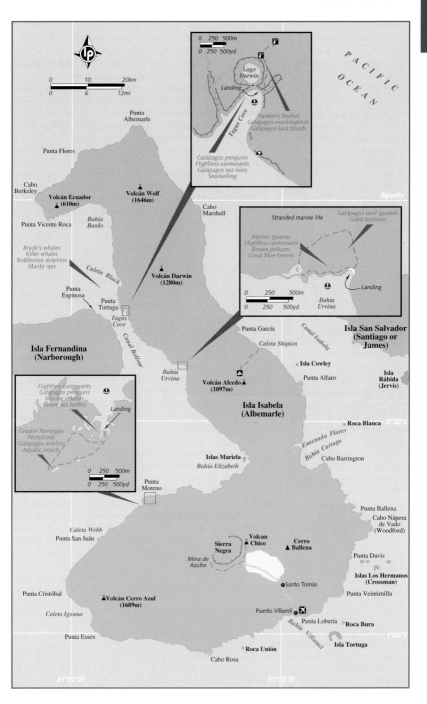

Punta Albemarle

Punta Flores

Cabo Berkeley

Volcán Ecuador (610m)

Punta Vicente Roca

Bahía Banks

Volcán Wolf (1646m)

Cabo Marshall

Equator

*Bryde's whales
Killer whales
Bottlenose dolphins
Manta rays*

Caleta Black

Punta Espinosa

Punta Tortuga

Tagus Cove

Volcán Darwin (1280m)

Tagus Cove

0 250 500m
0 250 500yd

Lago Darwin

Landing

*Darwin's finches
Galápagos mockingbirds
Galápagos lava lizards*

*Galápagos penguins
Flightless cormorants
Galápagos sea lions
Snorkelling*

PACIFIC OCEAN

Stranded marine life

*Galápagos land iguanas
Giant tortoises*

*Marine iguanas
Flightless cormorants
Brown pelicans
Great blue herons*

Landing

0 250 500m
0 250 500yd

Bahía Urvina

Isla San Salvador (Santiago or James)

Punta García

Caleta Shipton

Canal Isabela

Isla Cowley

Punta Alfaro

Isla Rábida (Jervis)

Isla Fernandina (Narborough)

Canal Bolívar

Bahía Urvina

Volcán Alcedo (1097m)

Isla Isabela (Albemarle)

*Flightless cormorants
Galápagos penguins
Marine iguanas
Green sea turtles*

Landing

*Greater flamingos
Waterbirds
Galápagos martins
Aquatic insects*

0 250 500m
0 250 500yd

Punta Moreno

Islas Mariela

Bahía Elizabeth

Roca Blanca

Ensenada Flores

Bahía Cartago

Cabo Barrington

Punta Ballena

Cabo Nápera de Vado (Woodford)

Caleta Webb

Punta San Juán

Sierra Negra

Volcan Chico

Cerro Ballena

Mina de Azufre

Santo Tomás

Punta Davis

Islas Los Hermanos (Crossman)

Punta Cristóbal

Volcán Cerro Azul (1689m)

Punta Veintimilla

Caleta Iguana

Puerto Villamil

Punta Lobería

Roca Bura

Punta Essex

Bahía Villamil

Isla Tortuga

Roca Unión

Cabo Rosa

0 10 20km
0 6 12mi

91°30'W

91°00'W

0°30'S

1°00'S

Location Puerto Villamil is 90km southwest of Puerto Ayora.
Facilities Airport, restaurants, basic services and giant tortoise breeding station at Puerto Villamil. Wet landings at Bahía Urvina and Caleta Shipton; dry landings at Tagus Cove and Punta Moreno.
Accommodation Hotels at Puerto Villamil.
Wildlife rhythms Female giant tortoises descend to Bahía Urvina during the wet months, December through March; Galápagos land iguanas begin breeding in January; waders best at Puerto Villamil November through March. Any of several volcanoes could erupt at any time.
Photo opportunities Giant tortoises, Galápagos land iguanas, Galápagos penguins, flightless cormorants, greater flamingos, Bryde's and killer whales, active volcanic fumaroles and craters.

Sally lightfoot crabs of different size and age show varied colouration at Punta Vicente Roca.

decorating the rocks. Watch also for **Galápagos penguins** and **marine iguanas**, and for **green sea turtles** surfacing in quiet reaches. The loop trail crosses a vast, empty swathe of lava, punctuated only with *mollugo* and lava cactus, which stretches up the slopes of Volcán Cerro Azul. Water-filled depressions fringed with vegetation make unlikely oases amid the desolation, but are rich in **aquatic insects**, which in turn attract **Galápagos martins** that hawk over the pools, and **waterbirds**, such as **greater flamingos, moorhens (gallinules), Galápagos pintails, egrets, herons** and **waders**.

Bahía Elizabeth has no landing; boats anchor offshore near the Marielas, two small islets with a scruffy crown of *palo santo* trees that are good for **Galápagos penguins, blue-footed boobies** and **red-billed tropicbirds**. Marine iguanas, Galápagos penguins and **flightless cormorants** perch on the rocky narrows at the lagoon entrance, **brown pelicans** nest in larger trees, and **great blue, striated** and **lava herons** hunt their prey along the edges. Young **Galápagos sea lions** laze about on low boughs of the larger mangroves, **green sea turtles** cruise through the shallows, and in quiet reaches you could see **golden** and **spotted eagle rays**. Look among the **ground-finches** and **small tree-finches** for **mangrove finches**; their presence has not been confirmed here for some years, but this is good habitat for this endangered species.

In 1954 a 6km strip of Isabela's west coast was uplifted 5m to 10m by volcanic activity, stranding coral, sea urchins and other marine life up to 1km inland. The new shoreline is accessible at Bahía Urvina, a short stretch of black sand flanked by rugged lava outcrops where **lava herons** hunt for **sally lightfoot crabs** among some very large **marine iguanas** and loafing **brown pelicans**. The trail inland heads towards the old coastline, now visible as a low cliff through dense stands of *palo santo* and *muyuyo*; feral pests, such as donkeys and goats, are common in this area. Female **giant tortoises** wander down from the slopes of Volcán Alcedo to nest and can usually be seen along the path during the wet season; they apparently relish the poisonous *manzanillo* (poison apple) fruits that grow along the trail. Some of the largest **Galápagos land iguanas** in the archipelago are resident here, emerging from their burrows as the day warms up. Small birds, such as **ground-** and **tree-finches**, and **yellow warblers**, forage in pairs or flocks, and **Galápagos mockingbirds** and **smooth-billed anis** are also common. Back at the beach, another path leads to a rocky point with brackish pools, mangroves and uplifted brain corals.

A Short Hop to Disaster

Because of the Galápagos' isolation and largely arid terrestrial environment, amphibians such as frogs and toads have never become established here. Amphibians have permeable skin that quickly dries out in the presence of sea water and thus cannot survive the sea-crossing from the mainland. But in 1998 a population of a small, brown tree frog, *Scinax quinquefasciata*, which is common in Ecuador, somehow became established in lagoons near Puerto Villamil. The frogs probably arrived as stowaways in cargo boats – tree frogs commonly hide in bunches of bananas – and their control is a top conservation priority for the GNPS and CDRS. Many amphibians are toxic to predators and although this species is not yet known to harm any native vertebrates, it multiplies quickly, preys on native insects and probably competes with native birds for food. Thousands of the frogs have already been removed from Puerto Villamil's lagoons by hand while other methods of control are being investigated.

Marine iguanas nest in the coarse sand and **Galápagos sulphur butterflies** flutter among the rock pools; a small colony of **flightless cormorants** nests at the point and there's usually a **great blue heron** hunting in the vicinity.

Botanic & Scenic Delights

Tagus Cove is well-protected by the slopes of two tuff craters and was used as an anchorage for up to 300 years by pirates, whalers and other seafarers. Ships' names dating from 1836 are carved on the rock and, far more recently, the steep cliffs have been extensively vandalised with illegal graffiti. **Flightless cormorants** sometimes nest above the landing dock among the **sally lightfoot crabs**, but a few always nest on rock platforms around the bay. The trail wends up a steep, dusty gully but **Galápagos sea lions** manage to haul themselves up to a cleft halfway, probably to avoid the biting flies down at sea level. An elevated boardwalk leads up to the rim of Lago Darwin (Lake Darwin), a landlocked crater with shallow, brackish water that attracts the occasional **Galápagos pintail** or **black-necked stilt**. The trail follows the lip of the crater through stands of large, silvery *palo santos* with scattered Galápagos croton and *muyuyo*; the mixed understorey includes a pioneering daisy tree quite unlike the towering scalesias that grow in the highlands. Birds seen along here include **woodpecker finches**, **large-billed flycatchers**, **smooth-billed anis** and **Galápagos mockingbirds**, among others, and **Galápagos hawks** keeping an eye out for Isabela's pale subspecies of **Galápagos lava lizard**. The best view over the lake is at the far side and the trail ends at a cinder cone with panoramic views of Volcán Darwin to the northeast.

A *panga* ride along the base of the cliffs is highly recommended for **Galápagos penguins**, **marine iguanas**, **sally lightfoots** and **Galápagos sea lions**; **common noddies** nest on ledges and in crevices just above the high-water mark and **Nazca boobies** sit higher up on the cliffs, especially outside the bay. Snorkelling is excellent in Tagus Cove, with playful sea lions, a good variety of **fish** including schools of **golden rays**, and a good chance at seeing Galápagos penguins and even **flightless cormorants** doing their thing underwater.

Just north of Tagus Cove, the long black sandy beach at Punta Tortuga has nesting **green sea turtles** and further north, almost on the equator, Volcán Ecuador is a small cone that has been eroded in half by the waves. **Swallow-tailed gulls** and **magnificent frigatebirds** wheel next to the steep, red-brown lava cliffs and up on Punta Vicente Roca there are hundreds of nesting **blue-footed boobies**.

Caleta Shipton, halfway down the east coast, is the landing for the ascent of Volcán Alcedo. The slopes and caldera rim of this quietly steaming volcano support the largest **giant tortoise** population in the Galápagos, but owing to a GNPS goat eradication program that was in place at the time of writing it is not possible for visitors to make the climb. This situation may change, so inquire with your tour operator when planning your trip. It's a fairly straightforward 10km hike from Caleta Shipton and it may be possible to extend the walk by another 12km once you get to the rim to reach the best tortoise area to the south. ■

Sunrise over Bahía Urvina.

Watching Tips
The dense stand of closed-canopy mangroves at Bahía Negra, north of Tagus Cove, is one of the only sites where the endangered mangrove finch is known to survive. Despite several searches in suitable habitat, it appears to be extinct on Fernandina and is known to exist in good numbers only at Tortuga Negra. However, you will probably have to charter a vessel to get there or join an organised bird-watching tour (p131).

SAN CRISTÓBAL (CHATHAM ISLAND)

Misty Highlands & Rugged Coasts

> ### Wildlife Highlights
> Galápagos sea lions, and endemic mocking-birds and lava lizards around the quiet port. Freshwater lagoons at El Junco support Galápagos pintails, moorhens (gallinules), black-necked stilts and pied-billed grebes. Punta Pitt is one of only two sites where all three boobies breed, as well as great frigatebirds, swallow-tailed gulls and Galápagos storm-petrels. Small population of giant tortoises at La Galapaguera. Great snorkelling with sea lions at Isla Lobos, where marine iguanas are easily observed feeding underwater. Wheeling seabirds and bottlenose dolphins at Roca León Dormido.

THE easternmost Galápagos island is also one of the oldest, an eroded volcano rising gently to moist highlands nearly 900m above sea level. Several endemic species and subspecies have evolved on San Cristóbal, but human impact has been severe over much of the island; the once extensive scalesia forest has been choked out by introduced guava and the miconia zone is a remnant of its former extent. Feral animals and intro-duced pests have contributed to the toll, and several native forms are now rare and others possibly extinct.

Nevertheless, conservation and rehabilitation programs are underway and a growing number of tour boats are op-erating out of Puerto Baquerizo Moreno, the sleepy capital of the Galápagos. Equally sleepy **Galápagos sea lions** flop over the rocks surrounding the harbour and, in the early morning before they are shooed away, on any boat's deck they can jump onto. The grounds of the Galápagos National Park Interpretation Centre, a few hundred metres north of the dock, are good for the endemic **Chatham mockingbird** (inset) and **San Cristóbal lava lizard**. **Yellow warblers**, **medium** and **small ground-finches**, **small tree-finches** and **large-billed flycatchers** can also be seen here and around town. The Interpretation Centre is the start of a short round-trip (2km) to Cerro de las Tijeretas (Frigatebird Hill), where both species of **frigatebird** can be seen thermalling beside the cliff, although they no longer nest at this site.

El Junco Lagoon is the only permanent freshwater lake in the Galápagos, and you can normally see **Galápagos pintails**, **moorhens (gallinules)** and **pied-billed grebes** here. The dense stands of miconia that once cloaked the slopes have largely been destroyed although habitat rehabilitation is underway. **Frigatebirds** visit El Junco to drink and bathe. It's also worth scanning across the large, ephemeral lagoon at the turn-off to El Junco for more **waterbirds**, such as **black-necked stilts**, moorhens and the possibility of a rarity. Look for **cattle egrets**, **bobolinks** and **whimbrels** in the surrounding fields.

Sea Wolves & the Sleeping Lion

Separated from San Cristóbal by a narrow channel, Isla Lobos is a small island that seems to be festooned with **Galápagos sea lions**. The GNPS dock is usually occupied by sleeping *lobos* (sea lions) and others rest in the shade of the solitary black man-grove that grows beside the channel. There's a short trail that involves a bit of boulder-hopping through saltbush and low *palo santo* punctuated with candelabra cactus. Nesting **blue-footed boobies** are abundant and other birds include **great frigate-birds** (there's a small colony of **magnificent frigatebirds** across the channel), **brown pelicans**, **lava gulls**, **common noddies**,

Mats of the endemic succulent sea purslane at Punta Pitt.

yellow warblers, and **small and medium ground-finches**. There's good snorkelling in the clear waters of the channel and this is one of the best sites to get in among sea lions underwater, keeping a wary eye on any territorial bulls. **Marine iguanas** are another highlight and you can safely watch them feeding among the jumble of submerged boulders. **Concentric puffers** and **Panama sergeant majors** gather in the shade of boats anchored above the channel's sandy bottom.

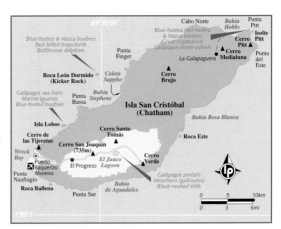

The seas around the north coast of San Cristóbal are a productive feeding area for seabirds, such as **boobies, waved albatrosses** and the three resident species of **storm-petrel**. All three species of booby nest side-by-side at spectacular Punta Pitt, an eroded volcanic cone at the island's northeastern tip, where the small, green-sand beach is littered with **Galápagos sea lions**. **Galápagos storm-petrels** nest on Isolte Pitt, a large sea stack just offshore, and the steep trail passes **swallow-tailed gulls** on cliffside nests, **great frigatebirds** and **red-footed boobies** nesting in low trees, and **Nazca** and **blue-footed boobies** on the ground, the larger Nazca boobies closer to the cliffs. **Small ground-finches** and **small tree-finches** forage with **Chatham mockingbirds** among ground vegetation.

About 1000 **Chatham giant tortoises** survive in the highlands of San Cristóbal and some can normally be seen at La Galapaguera. The long, hot trail starts at a sandy beach, where **green sea turtles** nest, and passes through arid-zone vegetation and signs of volcanic activity. The tortoises are normally seen around a crescent-shaped crater, Cerro Medialuna.

Roca León Dormido (Kicker Rock; below) is a 140m-high eroded tuff cone said to resemble a sleeping lion. The name's a bit of a stretch, but flocks of seabirds, such as **blue-footed** and **Nazca boobies**, frigatebirds and **red-billed tropicbirds** wheel around the massive sheer-sided cliffs. **Audubon's shearwaters** and **common noddies** feed nearby, and you should also watch for leaping **manta rays** and pods of **bottlenose dolphins**. ■

Location Easternmost island; 80km east of Puerto Ayora.

Facilities Puerto Baquerizo Moreno has Galápagos National Park Interpretation Centre, cafés, souvenir shops and services. Dry landings at Puerto Baquerizo Moreno and Los Lobos; wet landing at Punta Pitt.

Accommodation Hotels in Puerto Baquerizo Moreno.

Contact TAME (www.tame .com.ec; airport office), Cámara de Turismo (Tourist Information Office; www .galapagostour.org; Avenida Charles Darwin).

Wildlife rhythms Galápagos sea lions drop their pups during *garúa* season; red-footed boobies breed year-round at Punta Pitt.

Photo opportunities Galápagos sea lions, blue-footed and red-footed boobies, giant tortoises, endemic Chatham mockingbirds and lava lizards.

Watching Tips

To see San Cristóbal's endemic subspecies of vermilion flycatcher, ask your driver to stop at likely looking spots (such as large clumps of trees at the roadside) en route to El Junco Lagoon.

ESPAÑOLA (HOOD ISLAND)

Bigger, Brighter & a Whole Lot More

Wildlife Highlights

Sensational seabird viewing and the world's main breeding colony of waved albatrosses at Punta Suárez, plus accessible breeding Nazca and blue-footed boobies. Easily seen red-billed tropicbirds, Galápagos doves, swallow-tailed gulls, Galápagos hawks, and warbler and small ground-finches; one of only two sites for large cactus-finches. Galápagos sea lions and spectacular Hood marine iguanas in your face; and several endemic species, including Hood mockingbird, lava lizard and racer. Relaxing Bahía Gardner offers abundant sleeping sea lions, great snorkelling and close-up views of Galápagos hawks and Hood mockingbirds, among others.

ESPAÑOLA is thought to be an uplifted submarine lava flow and its location at the southeastern edge of the archipelago makes it one of the oldest islands. The island's surface tilts gently from vertical 30m to 100m cliffs on the southern coastline, which bears the brunt of prevailing southeast trade winds and the Pacific swell, to a low, sheltered north coast with a fine, sandy beach. Several unique species and subspecies have evolved here, including the **Hood giant tortoise**, whose rescue from the brink of extinction is a great Galápagos success story. At one point Española's entire giant tortoise population consisted of three males and 12 females, but after captive breeding at the CDRS (p91) more than a thousand hatchlings have been returned to the island, where they appear to be thriving.

Bahía Gardner features one of the longest beaches in the Galápagos, a 2km strip of white coral sand littered with supine female **Galápagos sea lions** and their at-times hyperactive consorts. Tracks of **green sea turtles** pock the dunes, while **sanderlings, ruddy turnstones, wandering tattlers** and **whimbrels** join resident **American oystercatchers** and beachcombing **Hood mockingbirds** on the sand. You can walk as far as the rocks midbeach, frequented by **marine iguanas** and **sally lightfoot crabs**, and up to the dense vegetation where **large-billed flycatchers, small ground-finches, warbler finches** and **large cactus-finches** forage and keep a wary eye out for **Galápagos hawks**. Look here also for the uncommon **Galápagos martin** and overhead for **great frigatebirds**. **Manta** and **spotted eagle rays** sometimes cruise offshore, and there's good snorkelling at Isla Tortuga, east of the bay, with **Mexican hogfish, yellow-tailed surgeonfish, Moorish idols, sea urchins** and occasional **white-tipped reef sharks**.

Bursting with Colour & Life

Depending on whether or not there's a bull **Galápagos sea lion** dozing on the dock, the landing at Punta Suárez is usually on a promontory of lava boulders that protects the sandy bay from rolling waves. Sea lions young and old play in the surf and lie on the beach, and you'll step over the Galápagos' most colourful **marine iguanas** (inset) on the rocky path. Some of these large lizards are truly spectacular, ranging from pink and turquoise to red and green, and many more are draped over the rocks among the **sally lightfoot crabs**. **Lava herons** hunt the fleet-footed crabs, **yellow-crowned night herons** shelter between boulders and **blue-footed boobies** often loaf near the park monument. The trail passes a small beach with more snoozing sea lions, abundant **Hood lava lizards** (the biggest and

Dozens of Galápagos sea lion cows laze about on Bahía Gardner's fine sandy beach.

most colourful species) and, as likely as not, a pair of **American oystercatchers** piping along the shore. You'll stop frequently among the waist-high saltbush, especially in the early morning when **Hood mockingbirds** perch high in the bushes, **Galápagos doves** forage at your feet and **Darwin's finches** and lava lizards bask on top of boulders.

Further along, the low cliffs are thronged with nesting **Nazca boobies** and more **marine iguanas**, which nest in a shingly patch at the foot of the cliff. This is one of the best

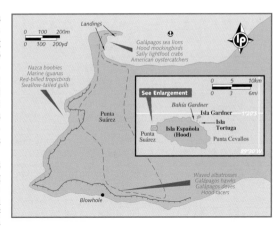

sites to see **red-billed tropicbirds** – they frequently wheel past the cliffs, although their nests are usually inaccessible over the edge; the nests of **swallow-tailed gulls** are easily seen, however. Heading inland, the trail crosses an expanse of low scrub, where **blue-footed boobies** nest in season, to a blowhole that shoots spray up to 25m into the air, depending on the tide (high tide is best). **Galápagos hawks** hunt in this area and mixed parties of **large cactus-** and **small ground-finches** pick among the bushes and rocks for seeds.

The blowhole (below) is an obligatory photo stop and the scenery is superb. Look out for **marine iguanas** and **Galápagos sea lions** enjoying the spray, and in season, **waved albatrosses** gliding into their nests or waddling to the precipice to launch themselves into the air. The albatross colony starts just beyond the blowhole – the trail doubles back at a prominent stack that's often adorned with **swallow-tailed gulls** and marine iguanas. The trail only skirts the edge of the colony through head-high vegetation, but you'll get an eyeful of these magnificent seabirds on their nests, courting or tending their huge, downy young. Here and elsewhere Española's three species of **Darwin's finch**, including **warbler finches**, are common and this rocky path is also one of the best sites to watch for **Galápagos doves** and the secretive **Hood racer**. **Galápagos hawks** nest in the vicinity and are usually easy to see. ∎

Location Isolated, southernmost island; 90km southeast of Puerto Ayora.
Facilities None. Wet landing at Bahía Gardner, dry landing at Punta Suárez.
Wildlife rhythms Waved albatrosses present at Punta Suárez late March until late December; green sea turtles nest at Bahía Gardner January through March.
Photo opportunities Waved albatrosses, Hood marine iguanas, Hood mockingbirds, Nazca boobies, red-billed tropicbirds, Hood lava lizards.

Watching Tips
Waved albatrosses caught at sea when the wind drops sit on the water in loose 'rafts', sometimes seen offshore from the cliffs at Punta Suárez.

FLOREANA (CHARLES ISLAND OR ISLA SANTA MARÍA)

Endemic Species & Underwater Riches

Wildlife Highlights

Must-visit island for birders to see endemic medium tree-finch, but endemic Charles mockingbird restricted to two offshore islands. Large colony of dark-rumped petrels in highlands. Punta Cormorant is one of the best sites in the Galápagos for greater flamingos, plus Galápagos sea lions, nesting green sea turtles, excellent wader-watching and endemic plants. Devil's Crown offers arguably the best snorkelling in the Galápagos, with some 50 fish species, Galápagos sea lions and great diving with hammerheads. Historic and novelty interest at Post Office Bay.

OFFICIALLY called Isla Santa María but known as Floreana (or Charles), this rugged island was formed by now-extinct volcanic activity and is old enough for several endemic vertebrates to have evolved here, such as the **Charles mockingbird**, **Floreana lava lizard**, **Baur's leaf-toed gecko**, **Floreana snake** and a subspecies of **giant tortoise**. Early settlers left a legacy of scandal, murder and intrigue, but their impact on Floreana's natural environment was disastrous. Galápagos hawks were persecuted to extinction; feral animals, such as donkeys, pigs and goats, contributed to the demise of giant tortoises, Galápagos land iguanas and large ground-finches; and the Charles mockingbird survives on only two small offshore islands, Champion and Gardner-by-Floreana.

Only a few human inhabitants still eke out a living in the hills and the tiny settlement of Puerto Velasco Ibarra. Even fewer tourists visit the highlands, but you should head for the hills if you want to seek out the endemic **medium tree-finch**. Unless you join an organised birding tour (p131), you will probably have to mount the search under your own steam, although the bird is not uncommon in the right areas. By basing yourself at the island's hotel you could walk up to suitable habitat in the early morning or ask around for a lift to the top of Cerro Paja and walk back down. Cerro Paja is also the breeding stronghold of the **dark-rumped petrel**, although the birds return to their nests only at dusk.

A large wooden barrel was placed at Post Office Bay in 1793 by British sailors to leave messages for homebound ships; the barrel has been replaced many times, but has been in more or less continuous use ever since. This site is mainly of novelty and historical interest, and if your boat doesn't stop here, there's a replica of the barrel in the Galápagos National Park Interpretation Centre at Puerto Baquerizo Moreno on nearby San Cristóbal (p80). The obligatory **Galápagos sea lions** dot the landing beach, **blue-footed boobies**, **brown pelicans** and **common noddies** roost on the rocky points and there's a lagoon east of the beach that sometimes attracts **greater flamingos** and **shorebirds**. A short trail leads past an abandoned fish-cannery to a lava tube that descends to sea level.

The lagoon at Punta Cormorant is one of the best sites in the archipelago for viewing the extraordinary greater flamingo.

The Pink & the Green

A few kilometres northeast of Post Office Bay, Punta Cormorant is near the northernmost tip of Floreana. Here, **Galápagos penguins** fish in the bay and loaf on the rocks, **red-billed tropicbirds** nest on the cliffs running north of the beach, and the landing beach (tinted green owing to the presence of the volcanic mineral olivine) is littered with sleeping **Galápagos sea lions**. But there are no cormorants; they have never lived on Floreana, and the site was named after a US naval vessel. However, Punta Cormor-

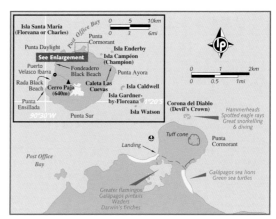

ant supports one of the biggest populations of **greater flamingos** in the Galápagos. As many as 150 flamingos use the site, mainly on the large, mangrove-fringed lagoon behind the beach, but they sometimes even strut along the sand among the sleeping sea lions. A short trail through the mangroves leads to the lagoon, which is also excellent for **waterbirds**. The flamingos' nests are visible on the far side and other avian inhabitants include **Galápagos pintails** and a roll call of **waders** such as resident **black-necked stilts** and migratory **whimbrels**, **willets**, **ruddy turnstones**, **phalaropes**, **semipalmated plovers**, **grey plovers**, **sanderlings**, **least sandpipers** and **wandering tattlers**. The vegetation behind the lagoon supports **Floreana lava lizards**, **yellow warblers**, **small** and **medium ground-finches**, and **small tree-finches**. A longer trail heads east round the north shore of the lagoon to a beach where **green sea turtles** haul up to nest.

Isla Onslow is the official name for a sunken cinder cone off Floreana's northern tip, but only the jagged, eroded rim protrudes above the waterline and it is far better known as Devil's Crown (Corona del Diablo). The 100m-wide crater has largely filled with sand and volcanic debris, and is only a few metres deep. The outside of the caldera walls drop away to at least 20m; irregular gaps form the prongs of the 'crown' and underwater caves link the

open sea with the crater. The warm shallows provide some of the best snorkelling in the islands, particularly near the eastern entrance. Some 50 fish species have been recorded, including **Moorish idols** and schools of **king angelfish**; other treats include **Galápagos sea lions**, large **marbled rays**, **white-tipped reef sharks**, **moray eels** and **green sea turtles**. Outside the caldera divers enjoy larger fry, such as **spotted eagle rays** and the main attraction, schools of **hammerheads** (inset). ■

Location Central island 55km south of Puerto Ayora.
Facilities None at visitor sites; wet landings at all sites except Puerto Velasco Ibarra.
Accommodation One hotel in Puerto Velasco Ibarra.
Wildlife rhythms Greater flamingos breed July through March; medium tree-finches may move to lowlands during dry months; dark-rumped petrels breed year-round.
Photo opportunities Medium tree-finches, greater flamingos, hammerheads, marine life.

Watching Tips
Puerto Ayora dive operators run day trips to islands off the Floreana coast, such as Champion, one of the only refuges of the Charles mockingbird.

FERNANDINA (NARBOROUGH ISLAND)

Life on the Edge

Wildlife Highlights
Pristine nature under an active volcano and a highlight of any cruise. Flightless cormorants, Galápagos penguins, Galápagos sea lions, waders and the world's largest colony of marine iguanas thrive on the edge of a barren lava flow. Fine stands of mangroves support yellow warblers, Darwin's finches, large-billed flycatchers, Galápagos hawks and nesting brown pelicans. Snorkellers can watch green sea turtles and marine iguanas underwater; and shallow lagoons attract sea turtles, more sea lions, fish and rays visible to landlubbers. Fine examples of lava cactus and pahoehoe lava.

EONS of uplifting and lava flows issuing from the massive domed cone of Volcán La Cumbre have formed Fernandina, the most volcanically active island in the Galápagos. Much of the island is made up of recent, barren lava flows, where life clings tenaciously to the rocky coast and a few fertile pockets on La Cumbre's slopes. A giant tortoise was found here in 1906 but none have been seen since and it is possible that they never became established. Fernandina can offer only a precarious existence for any animal as La Cumbre continues to grumble, spewing out lava on average every five years or so. The volcano's caldera floor collapsed in 1968, plummeting 350m, uplifts have made the landing dock at Punta Espinosa inaccessible at low tide, and at the time of writing La Cumbre was again erupting.

Punta Espinosa (Spiny Point) is a jagged promontory of cracked and eroded lava, but the name could also refer to the hundreds of spiny **marine iguanas** that drape the rocks. This is a large subspecies (males can measure up to 1.2m in length), dirty black with reddish tinges, that lines up in rows in the morning sun, eliminating excess salt by spurting it from their nostrils, or piles up under bushes to conserve body heat. **Swallow-tailed** and **lava gulls** greet landing parties on the rocks before a dense stand of red, white and black mangroves, used by **brown pelicans** for breeding and by **Galápagos hawks** as a lookout. **Yellow warblers** are common in the mangroves but also feed out among the tidal pools; and **warbler finches**, **small ground-finches**, **small tree-finches** and **large-billed flycatchers** also frequent the trees. Playful **Galápagos sea lion** (inset) pups frolic in rock pools or flop out on the mud between the mangrove roots at low tide.

The trail heads out to the point proper past large **marine iguana** breeding areas where, depending on the season, you could see females throwing up plumes of sand as they excavate nests, displaying to each other in warning and even fighting other females. **Galápagos sea lions** laze on various small beaches and **flightless cormorants** nest at the edge of the lava at the northern tip. **Waders** such as **wandering tattlers**, **whimbrels** and **American oystercatchers** pick over the rocks and sand for prey, **lava herons** poke among the rocks for the abundant **sally lightfoot crabs** and **Galápagos penguins** loaf on rocky platforms and islets, often in small groups.

A field of cracked pahoehoe lava, spewed out by Volcán La Cumbre, at Punta Espinosa.

Under the Volcano

The trail heading west takes you inland onto a lava flow that stretches up the slopes of Volcán La Cumbre. Fernandina's large, dark subspecies of **Galápagos lava lizard** scuttles among superb clumps of pioneering lava cactus that punctuate the black rock; and if you're lucky you might see a **Galápagos racer** in pursuit. Otherwise it is bare, although in the early morning or late afternoon you'll appreciate the austere beauty of swirls and eddies of pahoehoe lava, now solidified of course, and fields of razor-sharp aa lava rent by deep, brittle-edged fissures. Near where the trail ends a school of **yellowtailed** and **striped mullet** lives in a landlocked pool, which they probably entered as fry. Small cracks in the lava replenish the seawater, but the fish are now too big to escape through the narrow fissures. Keep an eye out for **Galápagos land iguanas** that live on the vegetated summit of La Cumbre and occasionally make their way down to Punta Espinosa, and for the **Galápagos doves** and **mockingbirds** that forage on the lava flows and among nesting seabirds on the point.

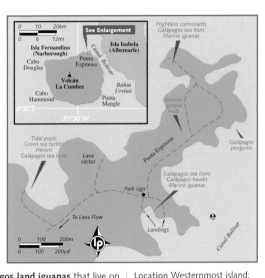

The large, mangrove-fringed tidal pools to the west of the point offer a shady contrast to the barren lava fields. **Galápagos sea lions** loll about, and **green sea turtles** – and an occasional **hawksbill** – probe the reaches. **Great blue** and **lava herons**, and **whimbrels** fish in these still pools; opportunistic **Galápagos hawks** perch on tall trees or drift overhead; and fish visible from the rocks include **Panama sergeant majors**, **whitetail damselfish** and **rays**.

Snorkelling around the rocks south of the anchorage is rather tame; for a real taste of life at the edge try snorkelling off the point, where the surge adds a frisson of excitement to watching **marine iguanas** (below), **green sea turtles** and if you're lucky, **flightless cormorants** underwater. Just offshore, expect to see both **Galápagos** and **Elliot's storm-petrels**, **blue-footed boobies**, **Audubon's shearwaters** and **common noddies**. Further out in the Canal Bolívar watch for **bottlenose dolphins**, **Bryde's whales** and occasional **killer whales (orcas)**, and **dark-rumped petrels** and **waved albatrosses**. ■

Location Westernmost island; 275km northwest of Puerto Ayora; 25km south of Punta Vicente Roca.

Facilities None; dry landing (wet at low tide) at the only visitor site.

Wildlife rhythms Marine iguanas breed January through June; flightless cormorants breed year-round; waved albatrosses in the Canal Bolívar April to December.

Photo opportunities Flightless cormorants, Galápagos penguins, marine iguanas, lava cactus, pahoehoe and aa lava.

Watching Tips
Birders should not expect to see the endangered mangrove finch at Punta Espinosa: it was last recorded here in 1974. For more information, see p76.

GENOVESA (TOWER ISLAND)

A Different Eden

Wildlife Highlights

Abundant breeding seabirds, including the world's largest colony of red-footed boobies, and some 200,000 pairs of nesting Galápagos storm-petrels. Large numbers of Nazca and blue-footed boobies, Audubon's shearwaters, red-billed tropicbirds and swallow-tailed gulls; many great and some magnificent frigatebirds. Galápagos sea lions plus easily seen Galápagos fur seals; the only island with two species of large-billed Darwin's finch (large ground-finch and large cactus-finch), plus sharp-beaked ground-finch and warbler finch. The smallest subspecies of marine iguana, but excellent snorkelling with good visibility. The best place to see short-eared owls.

A solitary egg blends in beautifully with the pebbly nest of a swallow-tailed gull.

THIS small, relatively flat island is the rim of a sunken crater that forms Bahía Darwin, a natural harbour 2.5km wide. Genovesa is geologically young (less than one million years old) and therefore some iconic Galápagos creatures, such as giant tortoises and land iguanas, have not yet become established. Similarly, snakes and lava lizards have yet to arrive, and otherwise widespread birds such as flycatchers, Galápagos hawks and barn owls are also missing. But it is the only island north of the equator that tourists are permitted to visit and is well worth the effort.

Lava gulls will probably be among the first birds you see, ever on the lookout for scraps near boats. Riding at anchor you'll be impressed by seabird activity on and around the cliffs: **red-footed boobies** returning to their nests, dozens of **great frigatebirds** thermalling overhead, **swallow-tailed gulls** along the shoreline, and **Audubon's shearwaters** and **red-billed tropicbirds** flying into nests in the sheer walls. Large schools of **golden rays** (up to 70 individuals) have been recorded feeding on the rich plankton in the bay and there's a good chance of seeing at least a few.

The cliffs also form a backdrop to a small beach at the northern edge of Bahía Darwin, where **Galápagos doves** and **Galápagos mockingbirds** forage among a few **Galápagos sea lions**. Small lagoons behind the landing are fringed with red mangroves where **yellow warblers**, **yellow-crowned night herons** and **Galápagos pintails** are common. A trail heads west past low saltbush with nesting **great frigatebirds**, **red-footed boobies** – look carefully for rare white-phase red-footed boobies here – and **swallow-tailed gulls** on their scrapes in the sand. The trail can be impassable at high tide, but there's usually a pair of **lava gulls** in this area, Genovesa's black **marine iguanas** drape the lava ridge west of the beach and **lava herons** stalk **sally lightfoot crabs**. You'll see plenty of Galápagos doves and Galápagos mockingbirds along the trail, and keep your eyes open for the four species of **Darwin's finch**: **large ground-** and **warbler finches** are common, **large cactus-finches** frequent the stands of opuntia, and Genovesa offers the best chance at seeing **sharp-beaked ground-finches**.

Stairway to Seabird Heaven

A rockfall near the tip of the caldera's eastern arm makes a natural staircase up the 25m cliff, usually referred to as Prince Philip's Steps or El Barranco. During the *panga* ride to the foot of the steps watch for **Galápagos sea lions** and **fur seals** sleeping on shady ledges; **marine iguanas** (Genovesa has the smallest subspecies), **common noddies** and **Galápagos mockingbirds** at the tideline; and the abundant **swallow-tailed gulls**. Overhead, a few **blue-footed boobies** nest precariously on the cliffs and **red-billed tropicbirds** dive into crevices, sometimes pursued by **great** or **magnificent frigatebirds**; Genovesa is a great island to watch the piratical frigatebirds harassing tropicbirds and boobies. **Galápa-**

gos doves feed among nesting **Nazca boobies** just inland from the top of the steps and, after the trail spans a deep crevasse in the lava, you'll come across **red-footed boobies** nesting on the *palo santo* trees. Genovesa supports some 140,000 pairs of red-footed boobies and their nests are spread all over the island. The trail winds through thick stands of *palo santo* and *muyuyo,* draped with more red-footed boobies, and interspersed with clearings where the Nazca boobies nest. The forest stops abruptly at a ridge of lava, beyond which is a barren field of broken lava punctuated by lava cactus. It's a bleak, forbidding landscape with a backdrop of bleached *palo santos,* but

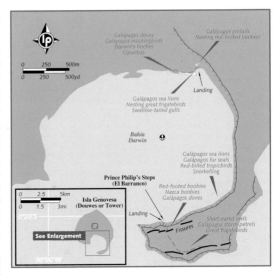

Galápagos doves
Galápagos mockingbirds
Darwin's finches
Opuntias

Galápagos pintails
Nesting red-footed boobies

Landing

Galápagos sea lions
Nesting great frigatebirds
Swallow-tailed gulls

Bahía
Darwin

Galápagos sea lions
Galápagos fur seals
Red-billed tropicbirds
Snorkelling

**Prince Philip's Steps
(El Barranco)**

Red-footed boobies
Nazca boobies
Galápagos doves

Landing

Short-eared owls
Galápagos storm-petrels
Great frigatebirds

Fissures

**Isla Genovesa
(Douwes or Tower)**

See Enlargement

some 200,000 pairs of **Galápagos storm-petrels** nest in holes and crevices under the crisp, fragile lava, and swarm above the flow. A deep fissure at the edge of the trail makes a shady roost for **short-eared owls** (below), and one can often be seen here (if not, just keep your eyes peeled along the trail – they actively hunt during the day for storm-petrels and young red-footed boobies). A smaller number of **band-rumped storm-petrels** also nests here among the Galápagos storm-petrels.

There's good visibility for snorkelling at the foot of the cliffs and with luck you'll be joined by a curious **Galápagos sea lion**. Pairs of **Moorish idols** are common, while schools of **yellow-tailed surgeonfish** drift among **Panama sergeant majors**, **king angelfish, white-banded angelfish, parrotfish, moray eels** and **dancer wrasses**. **White-tipped reef sharks** also cruise by and, in deeper water, **hammerheads** and **Galápagos sharks** are often seen. ∎

Location 125km north of Puerto Ayora.
Facilities None; wet landing at Bahía Darwin, dry landing at Prince Philip's Steps.
Wildlife rhythms Male great frigatebirds display March through June; red-footed boobies breed year-round; wet season brings a green flush to deciduous vegetation.
Photo opportunities Red-footed boobies, great frigatebirds, Galápagos storm-petrels, short-eared owls, reef fish.

Watching Tips
You'll see thousands of Galápagos storm-petrels, but most band-rumped storm-petrels arrive at dusk; watch for them at sea as you approach or leave Genovesa.

DAPHNE MAJOR

A Darwinian Magnifying Glass

Wildlife Highlights

Restricted site for a long-running study of four species of Darwin's finch (large, medium and small ground-finches, and cactus-finches) that has dramatically helped to prove Darwin's ideas on natural selection and support evolutionary theory. Sparsely vegetated but ideal for abundant breeding seabirds, including blue-footed and Nazca boobies, magnificent frigatebirds, red-billed tropicbirds, swallow-tailed gulls and brown noddies. Short-eared owls the only predator.

Location 50km north of Puerto Ayora.
Facilities None; dangerous wet landing; access restricted.
Wildlife rhythms Red-billed tropicbirds breed year-round; finch numbers fluctuate dramatically from 200 to 1000 between wet and dry seasons, and good and bad years.

Watching tips

Read J Weiner's Pulitzer Prize–winning *The Beak of the Finch* for an eloquent low-down on the remarkable research taking place on Daphne Major.

THIS steep, eroded tuff cone is surrounded by the Canal de San Salvador – so deep that boats cannot anchor – and accessible at only one point via a near-vertical cliff. Undercut by wave action, its distinctive outline protrudes 120m above sea level to a crater rim that surrounds a flat, open caldera floor. Vegetation is sparse and amounts to a few opuntias scattered among low *palo santo* trees and sprawling shrubs. But it makes a superb nesting site for the seabirds that wheel about the cliffs as you approach. Nests of **Nazca boobies** hug the cliff face and crater rim; **red-billed tropicbirds** nest in crevices, competing for sites with **short-eared owls**, **common noddies** and **swallow-tailed gulls**; and a colony of **blue-footed boobies**, numbering hundreds, occupies the crater floor, flanked by **magnificent frigatebirds** on the surrounding vegetation.

But Daphne is significant for another, far-reaching reason. In a unique experiment that has run for over 20 years, researchers have proved that the forces of evolution, far from being a nebulous concept, in fact occur subtly before our eyes every hour of the day. Teams of scientists have ringed, measured and studied all the **large**, **medium** (inset) and **small ground-finches** and **cactus-finches** on the island (bar one or two recalcitrants) in order to monitor their diet, behaviour and genetics. Bill shape is important in the choice of diet for Darwin's finches, and bill depth is critical for exerting enough force to crack the seeds upon which many species depend. By measuring the bill of every finch, the scientists found a high degree of individual  variation and overlap in bill depth between the three species of ground-finch. For example, the measurements of small individuals of the large ground-finch overlapped those of large specimens of medium ground-finch; and small specimens of medium ground-finch overlapped those of large specimens of small ground-finch.

During times of plenty, the various finches fed side-by-side on the wide range of seeds available on Daphne without specialising in a particular type. But in the aftermath of the disastrous 1983 El Niño, when food resources were pushed to the limit, bill size played a critical role in their survival. Only the stoutest bills of the large ground-finches could crack the hard seeds that survived the drought; and only the smallest of the small ground-finches were dextrous enough to extract tiny seeds previously left untouched from cracks and crevices; the birds least able to adapt eventually perished. The research showed that millimetre by millimetre, year by year, tiny, incremental adjustments in an animal's morphology spelt the difference between life and death when push came to shove. Over thousands of generations these vital differences cause profound and permanent changes to an animal's appearance, behaviour and ecology, and new species evolve. ∎

CHARLES DARWIN RESEARCH STATION

Conservation Behind the Scenes

The Charles Darwin Research Station (CDRS) was built next to Bahía Academy in Puerto Ayora in 1964 and now has a team of more than 200 scientists, educators, volunteers, students and staff dedicated to scientific research and environmental education. Its broad brief includes the monitoring and control of invasive species, marine research, restoring populations of giant tortoises, land iguanas and opuntias, and public education.

A boardwalk through towering opuntias takes you on a self-guided tour of visitor facilities, which include giant tortoise and land iguana breeding facilities, an interpretation centre, a library and a shop. Other facilities are for the use of scientists, staff and volunteers only, and are out of bounds to visitors.

There's a plan of the station near the entrance and it's worth dropping in to Van Straelen Hall, where illustrated display panels explain in simple terms the physical and living environment of the Galápagos, and introduce conservation and research themes; there's a short video presentation and station personnel give talks from time to time.

The tortoise breeding facilities include incubators, where you can view tiny hatchlings a fraction of the adults' size in climate-controlled conditions. Once the babies are large enough, they are released in progressively larger pens, shaded to protect the delicate juveniles from the intense sun, until they are approximately five years old, after which they are released into natural habitat on their respective native islands. Adult tortoises are kept in several corrals with low parapets that allow easy observation and photography. The largest corral can be entered by visitors, although you are asked to keep off the feeding platforms because of the risk of contaminating the tortoises' food supply.

The same incubators used for hatching tortoises are used to rear baby land iguanas; young land iguanas are sensitive to disturbance and most of their corrals are not open to the public, although several adults were on display at the time of research.

Behind the scenes at the CDRS, dozens of scientists and volunteers are engaged in studying Galápagos wildlife and ecosystems; implementing conservation programs; and educating the public, both locally and overseas through the CDRS website (www.darwin foundation.org; run by the Charles Darwin Foundation) and news releases. CDRS projects are carried out on land and under the sea, and include censuses of rare native plants and animals; eradication of weeds, such as blackberries, and invasive animals, such as black rats and goats; and the propagation and re-establishment of rare plants, such as the Española opuntia. International donors and sponsors help to fund these and many other projects, as well as the upkeep of facilities such as marine research vessels, laboratories and nurseries. The CDRS library houses the world's most comprehensive collection of references about the Galápagos and is open to the public, although the busy staff always appreciate it if you make an appointment first.

The CDRS is classed as one of the 54 Galápagos National Park Visitor Sites and a visit is highly recommended. Most tours include a visit to the station, but the CDRS is open to the public daily and you are also free to go there independently. Near the CDRS entrance there's a store selling souvenirs and CDRS products, including clothes, books, videos, posters, hats and other items; all profits are channelled back into the CDRS and its projects.

The excellent Charles Darwin Foundation website at www.darwinfoundation.org features news, updates and background information, and tells you how you can make donations or join the foundation. Opportunities sometimes arise for people who wish to volunteer their time or other resources to Galápagos conservation (check the website for details); although such opportunities are ultimately rewarding, be warned that field conditions in the Galápagos can be hot and uncomfortable, and work is generally conducted in Spanish. ∎

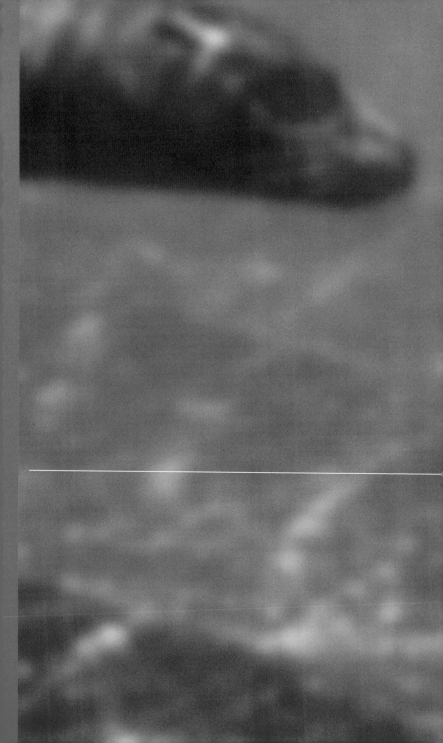

WILDLIFE GALLERY

*Recognising, Understanding &
Finding the Galápagos Islands'
Key Wildlife*

INTRODUCTION

THE tremendous geological and volcanic forces that formed the Galápagos archipelago have been shaping the earth for billions of years. A unique combination of circumstances created the wildlife that lives there: remoteness ensured that only a few land animals colonised the islands, and lack of competition from already existing forms allowed those that did arrive to evolve new shapes and behaviours, and to occupy empty ecological niches. Thus the familiar has been transformed into the bizarre, the commonplace into rarity and the islands' animal life is an unfamiliar mixture filling the same niches occupied by other species elsewhere.

The only land mammals that occur naturally on the islands are bats and native rats whose ancestors survived the crossing from South America. The arrival of bats presents no real mystery, but the rodents must have clung to floating vegetation – a process that is well-documented – until landfall. These adaptable small mammals became established on several of the islands, but you will be lucky to see either bats or rats.

Large marine mammals, however, are common and abundant. Sea lions and fur seals thrive in the rich waters of the Humboldt Current and visitors are almost guaranteed close and exciting interactions. While cruising between islands keep an eye out for dolphins and whales, which are seen regularly at certain times of year.

Even comparatively few birds managed to become established in the archipelago. Many of these are seabirds, such as boobies and frigatebirds, which are wide-ranging in tropical waters. But two seabirds in particular stand out: the graceful waved albatross – the world's only tropical albatross species – and the flightless cormorant, which lost the power of flight in the absence of land-based predators. Recent research in the Galápagos has confirmed what Charles Darwin suspected all along – that evolution works in tiny increments over vast periods of time to create the amazing animal and plant life we see

Previous page: An inquisitive Galápagos sea lion pup swimming in for a closer view at Puerto Egas, Santiago.

Right: Marine iguanas soaking up the sun at Punta Espinosa, Fernandina.

around us today. And there is no better example of this than the Galápagos finches – otherwise known as Darwin's finches – the small, rather nondescript birds that abound on every island. To a nonbirder these finches would scarcely rate a second glance (and even to bird-watchers their positive identification can be frustrating), but from a single ancestor they have radiated into various niches that would otherwise be occupied by other bird species. Their remarkable bill shapes and sizes fulfil a variety of feeding functions and one species, the woodpecker finch, has gone a step further by manipulating twigs or cactus spines to help it prise out grubs from under bark. The finch bears no relationship or resemblance to woodpeckers, which do not occur on the islands, but by adopting this remarkable behaviour it fills the same ecological role.

With lower metabolic needs, the 'cold-blooded' reptiles can survive on a poorer diet than the warm-blooded birds and mammals. Thus, the remarkable and unique marine iguanas can survive on seaweed and land iguanas on spiny cactus pads, both of which are nutritionally poor foods. Remoteness prevented large mammals, such as deer, from taking advantage of the abundant greenery in the highlands of several islands, but an equivalent ecological niche is filled by the famous giant tortoises, whose immense size enables them to survive the sometimes chilly mountain climate.

Like possibly no other place on earth the Galápagos Islands guarantee close encounters of the wildlife kind. Your visit will allow you to witness first-hand the remarkable wildlife that led Charles Darwin to have what has been described as 'the best idea anyone ever had'. Of course, modern visitors are privileged to have more than 150 years of thought and scientific research to help explain what they see, but treat your visit like a detective story and try to figure out for yourself some of the interactions between the unique animals and plants that first piqued Darwin's curiosity. ■

GALÁPAGOS FUR SEAL

Recognition Bulls blackish or dark brown, usually with contrasting mane; cows paler brown. Short, blunt head with nose more pointed than sea lion. Bulls 65–80kg, up to 1.6m in length; females about 27kg, up to 1.3m in length.
Habitat Rocky shores of marine coasts adjacent to deep water; mostly in western islands.
Behaviour Males mature at 5–6 years, become territorial at 9 and remain dominant for about 3 successive years. Copulate on land.
Breeding Single pup dropped during *garúa* season (usually October) on average every 2 years. Pups moult into adult fur at about 5 months, first feed independently at 6–7 months.
Feeding Mostly nocturnal; dives up to 100m for squid and lantern fish rising towards the surface.
Voice Rarely heard; similar to sea lion but less vocal and more guttural.
Spanish *Lobo de los pelos.*

Back from the Brink

It is easy to think of the endemic Galápagos fur seal as rare, because most visitors encounter it at only a few sites, where its behaviour is much more retiring than the extroverted Galápagos sea lion. But although it was hunted almost to extinction in the 19th century, the fur seal has bounced back under protection and now numbers between 25,000 and 40,000 animals – making it almost as abundant as the ubiquitous sea lion. This is the smallest of the world's seven species of fur seal and is noticeably smaller than the Galápagos sea lion, but although size is a useful identification feature, to the inexperienced eye the fur seal is hard to differentiate. Behaviour is a good clue: fur seals have thick, luxurious fur – the reason for their massive overexploitation by humans – and avoid the hot sun by resting in shady crevices and under rocky overhangs. For the same reason, fur seals usually avoid body contact with others, unlike Galápagos sea lions. A thick coat may seem like an encumbrance in the tropics, but it's a trait Galápagos fur seals inherited from a subantarctic ancestor; and besides, they are nocturnal hunters that feed in deep, cold waters, particularly on the outer edges of islands where upwellings provide rich pickings. Up close, note their large, bulging eyes, with a distinctly glazed look, proportionally large foreflippers and tiny button nose.

Fur seals aren't 'true' seals at all: they are closely related to sea lions and, like them, have external ears and propel themselves underwater with their foreflippers. In fact, some guides call them fur sea lions, and this is probably a more accurate name. The fur seal's stronghold is in the west of the archipelago, where they form small colonies on every island but are rarely seen at sea. Their smaller size means they can haul out onto steeper, rockier shores than sea lions and at Puerto Egas, on Santiago, they sleep high on the cliffs. Bulls are highly territorial and aggressive during the mating season (August to November); females come into oestrus only a few days after giving birth and competition for mating opportunities is fierce. Galápagos fur seal pups have the longest suckling period of any pinniped – two years or more. ∎

Hotspots
Santiago (Puerto Egas), **Genovesa**

GALÁPAGOS SEA LION

Beach Bums & Underwater Ballerinas

Formerly regarded as a subspecies of the widespread California sea lion, Galápagos sea lions are found on every island and are thought to have a population of about 50,000. You will see them at virtually every site, porpoising through the water next to your *panga* (dinghy) or dozing on a smooth surface such as the concrete dock where you expect to land. Females and pups are easy to step around, but territorial bulls sometimes force visitors to make a wet landing (don't be alarmed, but do follow your guide's instructions). Underwater, sea lions are inquisitive and playful – especially the pups – and snorkelling with these streamlined animals will be one of the highlights of your trip to the Galápagos.

Sea lions seem to spend a lot of time lounging around, strewn across sandy beaches or lolling in the shallows. But these apparently lifeless lumps can make an amazing transformation into lithe masters of surf and swell, and are superbly adapted for underwater hunting, using their foreflippers for propulsion and hind for steering. Mature bulls are much larger than cows and can weigh up to twice as much. They need all that muscle and brawn to fight off rivals as they try to dominate stretches of beach where the cows haul out to sleep: he who can protect the most desirable stretch of sand will earn the right to mate with the cows that use it. After mating, the beachmaster has nothing more to do with his offspring, but don't underestimate these beach bums – sea lions can move fast on land and you won't want to risk a tangle with a territorial bull either in or out of the water. Spent bulls congregate in 'bachelor' colonies away from the female haul-outs, dozing away a life less stressful. Cows spend the first week of their pup's life bonding with it; after this phase she hunts by day and suckles the pup by night. At five weeks the pup moults its baby coat (lanugo) and looks more like an adult; at five months it begins to feed inshore, although it may be dependent on the mother for some time after. ■

Recognition Bulls dark brown, black when wet; up to 2.3m long with thick neck, steeply sloping forehead and raised crown. Cows creamy brown with doglike muzzle.
Habitat Sandy shores and rock platforms of marine coasts; sometimes seen at sea.
Behaviour Highly thigmotactic, sleeping in groups or piles. Nonbreeding males form bachelor groups. Females sexually active at 3 years, males fully mature at 10. Cows come into oestrus and copulate 3–4 weeks after pupping.
Breeding A single pup (rarely twins) usually born in *garúa* season (June to November). Breeding season varies between islands.
Feeding Fast and efficient diurnal hunters of fish (especially sardines).
Voice High-pitched barks and yelps.
Spanish *Lobos.*

Hotspots
Plaza Sur, **Isla Mosquera**, **Española** (Bahía Gardner), **Santa Fé**, **Rábida**, **Santiago** (Puerto Egas)

BOTTLENOSE DOLPHIN

Recognition Variable grey upperparts can appear uniform but may actually be several shades; paler below. Prominent dorsal fin, bulging forehead, short beak. Length 3–4.2m; males larger.
Habitat Coastal and pelagic waters, including bays, sometimes close to shore.
Behaviour Pod composition and stability varies; bands of related females may stay together for years.
Breeding A single calf born underwater after a year's gestation is suckled another year and weaned at 18–20 months. Calves born year-round; can associate with mother for years after weaning. Females can still breed at 45 years.
Feeding Mainly fish and invertebrates inshore, pelagic fish and squid offshore; also takes injured fish and some offal around trawlers.
Voice Silent apart from echolocation underwater.
Spanish *Delfin mular.*

The Ubiquitous Toothed Whale

Your boat's crew will usually let you know when a cetacean (whale or dolphin) is spotted from the bridge and bottlenose dolphins are the most commonly sighted species in Galápagos waters. You'll never tire of watching these small toothed whales, and their playful and inquisitive nature has made them the favourite of aquaria the world over. Watch for distant splashes and the telltale dorsal fin as they break the surface to breathe through their single blowhole (dolphins don't normally show a spout like larger whales). This is the cetacean most likely to ride a boat's bow-wave and with luck you'll be joined by a pod, seemingly in a race to ride the slipstream directly under the prow. In fact, bottlenoses can be belligerent, jostling each other for a prime spot under the bow and even knocking smaller species out the way. Their famous antics are not restricted to captivity and in the wild they frequently leap (breach) several metres clear of the water or even turn somersaults; one prosaic explanation for this exuberance is that they may be trying to rid themselves of parasites, but they could just be having fun. They also ride waves in the wake of vessels, ride the pressure waves of large whales and surf in breakers near the shoreline.

Bottlenose dolphins are found the world over in all but polar waters and are the largest of the typical dolphins. Pods usually number 20 to 30 individuals and typically feed co-operatively, although individuals are occasionally seen hunting alone and bottlenoses frequently associate with other species, such as common dolphins and short-finned pilot whales. If they ignore your boat it may be because they have other fish to fry: several pods may congregate at fish shoals, and be joined by plunge-diving pelicans and boobies and even sharks at the feeding frenzy. Sharks, however, are the main predator of dolphins, and individuals often show scarring from shark attacks. Bottlenoses have a varied diet, taking prey from the sea bottom inshore and diving as deep as 500m offshore. One of their most remarkable behaviours is 'fish whacking', whereby they stun fish with their tail flukes. ∎

> **Hotspots**
> **Canal Bolívar**,
> **San Cristóbal** (Roca
> León Dormido)

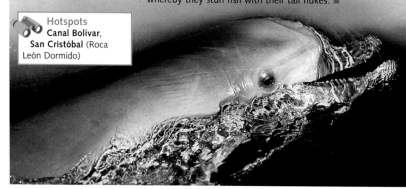

KILLER WHALE

Gregarious Killers

Of the 25 species of whale and dolphin recorded in Galápagos waters, the killer whale (orca) is undoubtedly the most spectacular. This is the world's most widespread cetacean; sightings around the archipelago are relatively common and could occur in virtually any stretch of ocean. The killer whale is actually a species of dolphin – the largest, in fact – and one of the so-called 'blackfish', a group of species that includes pilot whales and other large, black 'dolphins'. Like its smaller relations it is one of the toothed whales, carnivores that prey on vertebrates, unlike the plankton-feeding great or baleen whales. Until as recently as the 1960s killer whales were persecuted because they were considered a danger to humans. However, there has never been an authentic case of an attack on humans, and research on captive orcas has shown them to be highly intelligent.

Recognition Unmistakable if seen well; black with white eye-patch, white underparts and grey saddle. Rounded head, paddle-shaped flippers. Length 5.5–9.8m; males' dorsal fin up to 1.8m high.

Habitat Cool marine waters from surf zone to open sea, usually within 800km of coast.

Adult males are usually solitary, but females form groups of up to nine related individuals from up to four generations of matrilineal descent. These groups band together in stable, sociable pods of up to 60 animals that travel, hunt and play together, with all members helping to raise the calves. Closely related pods, known as clans, develop their own dialect of underwater noises and some appear to specialise in specific prey. Killer whales are idiosyncratic near boats, sometimes approaching with apparent curiosity but often ignoring them, although they frequently show behaviours such as breaching, spy-hopping and slapping the water with flukes and flippers.

Behaviour Pods normally of 3–25 animals; superpods of 150 may form. Sometimes associates with other cetaceans without harming them. Blow low and bushy.

Breeding Calving occurs year-round at an average interval of 5 years per female. Single calf born underwater after 15–18 month gestation is nursed for 1 year and fully weaned at about 2 years.

No toothed whales are more voracious than killer whales on the hunt. Travelling at up to 55km/h, pods often cooperate to surround prey, such as a school of fish or other whales, and consolidate to drive bait fish into tight balls which they then take bites out of. Their food tastes are eclectic; prey includes school fish, sea turtles, seals, seabirds, other whales (including the tongues of young baleen whales) and even land animals caught crossing water. Killer whales appear to be most abundant when their favourite prey is about, such as when fish are spawning and seals are pupping. ∎

Feeding Prey ranges from fish, birds and squid to sea turtles, seals, dolphins and even great whales.

Voice Silent apart from underwater echolocation.

Spanish *Orca*.

Hotspots
Canal Bolívar

GALÁPAGOS PENGUIN

Recognition Black upper-parts, including flippers, with white edging to face; dirty white underparts. Pink lower and black upper mandible; dirty pink feet. Brown eyes. Length 50cm.

Habitat Inshore marine waters near nutrient upwellings; loafs on rock platforms.

Behaviour Sedentary; adults mate for life, breeding in pairs or loose colonies of up to 40 birds. Sometimes feeds cooperatively in groups of 50–200 birds. Young and some adults disperse to other islands after breeding.

Breeding 1–2 eggs laid in crevices near sea level are incubated 38–42 days; normally only 1 chick raised; fledges at 60 days.

Feeding Pursues pelagic school fish up to 15cm long underwater; common prey includes sardines and mullet.

Voice Loud, donkeylike braying frequently uttered near nest when breeding.

Spanish *Pingüino de las Galápagos.*

The World's Only Tropical Penguin

All penguins are flightless and most species are restricted to the southern continents and subantarctic waters, but the Galápagos penguin lives permanently in the tropics and is the only species to do so. Its ancestor – a likely contender is the peripatetic Humboldt penguin, which it closely resembles – probably followed the cold Humboldt Current north and, finding a year-round food supply, became established in the archipelago. But life on the equator means overcoming some of the very traits that enable other penguins to survive in one of the earth's coldest regions. Thus, to avoid overheating in their superbly insulated plumage, Galápagos penguins have evolved the shortest feathers of any penguin, and can tolerate water temperatures of up to 28°C. Their Antarctic cousins nest on bare ground to allow whatever sunshine is available to help incubate their eggs, but this behaviour would be counterproductive under the fierce tropical sun, so the Galápagos penguin incubates its eggs in shady crevices.

Galápagos penguins are unmistakable on land, with an upright stance and an ungainly walk with flippers akimbo. When swimming, their ungainliness disappears and penguins 'fly' through the water, in bursts of up to 35km/h, by flapping their flippers (actually rudimentary wings) and steering with their feet and tail in pursuit of fish. They can readily be spotted loafing on exposed rock platforms at a few visitor sites, but the Galápagos Islands are the only place on earth where you can watch penguins feeding underwater without sophisticated equipment. In fact, snorkellers may be used as a barrier against which a penguin herds a school of fish (divers in wetsuits are usually avoided because they resemble sea lions – one of the penguins' main predators).

Galápagos penguins suffered a massive decline during the 1982–83 El Niño, the population falling from an estimated 6000 to 15,000, to fewer than 500 birds in 1984. Numbers began to climb again in 1985 (Galápagos penguins can nest year-round and sometimes raise two clutches in a year) and are on the rise once again. But these birds are still vulnerable to attacks by feral dogs, cats and rats, and another severe El Niño season could make them seriously endangered. ■

Hotspots
Isabela (Tagus Cove), **Fernandina** (Punta Espinosa), **Bartolomé** (Pinnacle Rock)

FLIGHTLESS CORMORANT

A Highly Unusual Seabird

Cormorants of several species, collectively numbering millions, live in colonies along the west coast of South America, but cormorants are not normally found on oceanic islands (in fact, they are rarely seen out of sight of land) and their presence in the Galápagos archipelago is unusual enough. Somehow they became established here, and in the absence of land-based predators they became the world's only flightless cormorant. The flightless (or Galápagos) cormorant is also the world's largest cormorant, but in nearly every other way it is typical of cormorants everywhere. Cormorants dive to the sea floor to hunt, and to decrease their natural buoyancy their feathers lack waterproofing. They must regularly leave the water to dry their plumage and this is when they adopt a characteristic pose – perched semi-upright with wings held out to the side. Flightless cormorants also show this behaviour, even though their wings have dwindled to about the size of a penguin's flippers. Even their flight muscles are rudimentary: when pursuing prey underwater, Galápagos cormorants hold their wings close to the body and propel themselves with their large webbed feet and stout legs, using the tail for steering. But they use their wings to balance as they hop from rock to rock, and during courtship pairs flutter their wings while circling each other in a spiral rising through the water.

Flightlessness is very unusual among seabirds and evolved most commonly among land birds on oceanic islands. But wherever exotic predators have been introduced to these islands, the 'ecologically naive' flightless species were usually the first to be exterminated. Indeed, the naturally rare flightless cormorant suffers from predation by feral dogs on Isabela and has been fortunate to survive into the 21st century: the 1982–83 El Niño halved its population, although after 1985 it was able to recover to its previous population of about 900 to 1200 pairs. This was partly due to the fact that it is able to raise two broods in a year, as females leave the males to finish rearing the young while they start a new brood. However, this remarkable bird occupies a precarious niche and is still vulnerable to disturbance by tourists and commercial fishing. ■

Recognition Entirely black-brown with turquoise eyes; large head, vestigial wings and big, webbed feet. Length 100cm, weight 2.5–4kg; males up to 1kg heavier than females, with heavier bill.
Habitat Cold inshore marine waters associated with Cromwell Current; nests above tide limit on rocky coasts.
Behaviour Sedentary; rarely moves far from breeding site or between islands. Forms small breeding groups of up to 12 pairs. Builds large seaweed nest lined with flotsam; males present females with seaweed when returning to nest.
Breeding 2–3 eggs laid year-round but mainly March to September; incubation 35 days. Normally only 1 chick raised; fledges at 60 days.
Feeding Dives for benthic animals, such as eels, rock fish, octopuses and squid, which it pursues underwater.
Voice A low growl; nestlings give a plaintive wee-wee.
Spanish *Cormorán mancón, cormorán no volador, pato cuervo.*

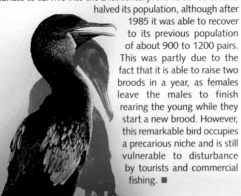

Hotspots
Fernandina (Punta Espinosa), **Isabela** (Tagus Cove, Bahía Urvina)

BROWN PELICAN

Ungainly on Land, Graceful in the Air

Pelicans are instantly recognisable with their massive pouched bill, and are a familiar sight along the coast of every large island. Although they are often seen loafing on the dock at Puerto Ayora, pelicans are clumsy and vulnerable on land, and being among the heaviest of flying birds they require a runway – land or water – to gain momentum for takeoff. But once airborne they are elegant and acrobatic: like the related frigatebirds they commonly soar on thermals, but can also glide inches off the water's surface. Flocks typically fly in a V-formation, with each bird flapping then gliding in turn. Brown pelicans are the only pelicans that regularly feed by plunge-diving: selecting a fish from as high as 15m, they plunge headfirst with mouth open and wings folded, thrusting back the wings and feet just before impact to increase speed. Dozens may plunge-feed on shoals of fish, sometimes in the company of other seabirds such as blue-footed boobies, and may even follow shoals close inshore, diving into water a few feet deep without apparent harm. This is the only pelican species that will follow fishing (and tour) boats, hoping to snatch some of the offal thrown overboard; young birds in particular perch on the rails of moored boats and even plunge-dive for fish attracted to lights at night. ∎

Recognition Unmistakable; grey-brown overall with white head and throat, and chestnut hindneck. Wingspan 2m.
Habitat Coastal waters.
Behaviour Doesn't usually fish cooperatively.
Breeding Breeds year-round; builds stick nest in bushes or trees. Nestlings fledge at 63–75 days.
Feeding Fish, shrimps.
Voice Adults normally silent.
Spanish *Pelicano café.*

Hotspots
Santa Cruz (Puerto Ayora), **Rábida**, **Isabela** (Bahía Elizabeth)

RED-BILLED TROPICBIRD

'Twixt Booby & Tern

The three species of tropicbird inhabit tropical and subtropical waters, although only the red-billed tropicbird occurs in the Galápagos. These graceful birds are instantly recognisable by the long tail streamers that account for half their body length and trail behind them in flight. The streamers play a role in courtship displays, but they are constantly being damaged or broken and regenerate throughout a bird's life. They also earned tropicbirds the alternative name of bosunbird, after the marlinspikes (pointed metal tools) carried by boatswains (or bosuns) on sailing ships. Although they resemble an outgrown tern, tropicbirds are related to pelicans and boobies, and like them plunge-dive for fish, sometimes from as high as 25m. They are usually solitary, feeding far out to sea and are able to fly great distances without stopping. Cliffs offer the best vantage points for watching tropicbirds, and their flying ability is best appreciated during courtship: groups perform noisy synchronised flights before pairs break off and fly in unison, banking, gliding and touching their tails. Sea cliffs also provide the best nesting sites and, although they breed in loose colonies, tropicbirds fight fiercely over nest sites and even usurp the nests of other species. With short legs, they can hardly walk; cliffs give them the elevation to become easily airborne while shady nooks protect their young from predators. ∎

Recognition White with black wing tips, eyestripe and vermiculated ('waved') back; red bill.
Habitat Coastal cliffs, pelagic waters.
Behaviour Feeds up to 1500km from land; rarely approaches boats.
Breeding 1 egg incubated for 42 days; chick flies at 70–90 days.
Feeding Flying fish, squid.
Voice Shrieks.
Spanish *Ave tropical.*

Hotspots
Genovesa, **South Plaza**, **Española** (Punta Suárez)

GREAT FRIGATEBIRD

Consummate Aerial Pirates

Few birds can match the aerial supremacy of frigatebirds and these huge black birds spend much of their waking life on the wing. There are two very similar species in the Galápagos, the great frigatebird and the magnificent frigatebird; males are almost identical and an experienced eye is needed to identify females and juveniles. Also known as man-o-war birds, frigatebirds are most famous for waylaying other seabirds, such as blue-footed boobies and red-billed tropicbirds, as they return to their nests after a day's fishing. With a streamlined body, massive wingspan and ultralight bones, frigatebirds are highly manoeuvrable and harass other birds in midair – often grabbing them by the tail – until they drop or regurgitate their catch, which they then scoop up in midflight. This form of piracy is known as kleptoparasitism, but in fact less than 20% of their food may be obtained in this way. Dozens of frigatebirds float effortlessly high on thermals above their colony at dawn, before drifting far out to sea to spend the day feeding. They expertly snatch fish from the surface without landing or diving and readily join dolphins, tuna and other seabirds at feeding frenzies. Frigatebirds are adept at snatching flying-fish in midair and, ever opportunistic, congregate to feast on waves of baby sea turtles hatching on beaches.

All frigatebird species have a long breeding cycle, which begins with an extraordinary courtship display. Males have a naked throat patch, called a gular pouch, that is normally almost invisible. At the start of the breeding season males sit on top of vegetation, cock their great wings and inflate their scarlet pouch like a balloon. When females fly overhead, they vibrate their whole body, uttering a cowlike mooing while vibrating bill against pouch. Eventually a female can no longer resist this unlikely beacon and pairs up with an attractive male. Parental care is intense and lasts up to a year or more after the chick fledges, during which young birds must learn the subtle fishing techniques carried out far to sea. Juvenile mortality is high and the main culprits of kleptoparasitism are probably young frigatebirds near colonies trying to avoid starvation. ∎

Recognition All black, males with green sheen to back feathers, females with white breast and pale-red eyering; juveniles with white head and rusty breast. Wingspan 2.2m.

Habitat Aerial except at breeding colonies, pelagic and coastal; nests on bushes or trees.

Behaviour Often perches on boats. Drinks fresh water when available; bathes in flight. Males break off or steal branches in flight; females build nest. Cools off by spreading and inverting wings. May sleep on the wing at sea.

Breeding Biennial; 1 egg incubated by both parents for 42 days; young fledge at about 90 days.

Feeding Mainly fish caught at sea, especially flying-fish; also squid, jellyfish, sea-turtle hatchlings, seabird eggs and chicks. Robs seabirds of catch in flight.

Voice Usually silent; males make a drawn-out *oo-oo-oo* when displaying.

Spanish *Fragata común.*

Hotspots
North Seymour, Genovesa, San Cristóbal (Punta Pitt)

*Large size, striking black-and-white plumage and a yellow bill readily identify the **Nazca booby**.*

*The brown-phase **red-footed booby** outnumbers white-phase birds by about twenty to one.*

*Red feet and a bluish bill simplify the identification of the white-phase **red-footed booby**.*

BOOBIES

The Fine Art of Communal Living

The bird order that includes pelicans, cormorants, tropicbirds and frigatebirds is well represented in the Galápagos, both in species and numbers, and one other family, the boobies, is particularly conspicuous. Boobies are closely related to gannets and share their teardrop-shaped body, conical bill and plunge-diving feeding strategy. Their unflattering name came about because seafarers found them easy to kill at their nests. Not surprisingly, the Galápagos is one of the few places left on earth where boobies can still be approached closely.

The blue-footed booby (inset) is typical of the family, with spectacular webbed feet whose amazing colour makes it easily identified (at least in adult birds). In one of the most comical courtship displays in the bird world, pairs lift their feet one at a time and wave them in the air. All boobies plunge-dive from great heights into shoals of fish like airborne torpedoes, and blue-footed boobies may be encountered feeding just about anywhere in Galápagos waters, at sea or close inshore, and even in harbours.

But in fact the blue-footed booby is the least numerous of the three species in the Galápagos and is greatly outnumbered by the most abundant, the red-footed booby, which numbers some 250,000 pairs. This is the species least often seen by visitors because it nests at only a few remote locations where it is safe from predation by Galápagos hawks. Adults are easily recognised, although there are two plumage variations: a brown one that makes up 95% of the Galápagos population and a striking black-and-white morph. The third, and largest, species is the Nazca booby. Formerly regarded as a subspecies of the masked booby, the Nazca booby is now recognised as a full species; the Galápagos, with some 25,000 to 50,000 pairs, is the core of its range.

Since such vast numbers of seabirds must tax the resources of even the Humboldt Current, the three boobies coexist by partitioning available food: each feeds on slightly different fish species or in different marine zones, the red-footed booby feeding farthest from shore. Each booby also occupies a different breeding niche to avoid direct competition for space: the red-footed, the smallest, is light enough to nest in trees and bushes; the blue-footed nests on the ground; and the Nazca occupies ground sites near cliffs where takeoff is simply a matter of launching into the air. ■

> **Hotspots**
> **Española** (Punta Suárez) Breeding colonies of Nazca and blue-footed boobies. **Genovesa** World's largest red-footed booby colony, including a few of the black-and-white morph. **San Cristóbal** (Punta Pitt) The three booby species breeding side-by-side show partitioning of nest sites.

*Although the **blue-footed booby** is the most easily seen booby in the Galápagos, it is the least abundant.*

WAVED ALBATROSS

Driven by the Wind

Most albatrosses live in the storm-lashed southern oceans, where their slender wings enable them to glide effortlessly over the air currents caused by oceanic rollers. They rarely cross the equator, where the winds are unreliable, but one remarkable species, the waved albatross, nests on Española and is the only albatross that breeds in the tropics. Galápagos waters provide an abundant food supply for what is effectively the world's entire population (about 12,000 breeding pairs, although there are also 10 to 50 pairs on Isla La Plata, Ecuador). Albatrosses need winds of at least 18km/h to stay aloft and the breeding of waved albatrosses is tied rigidly to the trade winds that blow between March and December. During the warmer months, January and February, they disperse into the Humboldt Current off Ecuador and Peru and are virtually unknown in Galápagos waters. These huge birds need a runway to become airborne and only Española provides open, flat areas near high cliffs that face into the prevailing winds; takeoff is achieved either by running into the wind or by simply dropping off the cliff and opening their great wings.

Waved albatrosses pair for life, males returning to Española at the end of March to establish breeding territories. After months at sea, pair bonds must be re-established with the returning females and pairs have evolved an elaborate ritual that includes a swaggering gait, mooing and complex movements, such as bill-circling and -clapping, sky-pointing and gaping. Inexperienced pairs perform rather inept routines, but if you are lucky enough to see a well-established pair go through their paces it's a mesmerising sight. Large, loose colonies form in open areas and the first eggs are laid by mid-April. A growing chick's food requirements are huge and adults commonly spend days at sea fishing while the downy chicks gather in crèches. Returning every few days, adults find their chick by calling and regurgitate up to 2kg of partly digested food and stomach oil at a time. The last of the year's young leave at the end of January and juveniles may stay at sea until breeding age. ∎

Recognition Grey-brown back and belly separated from white head and neck by fine vermiculations ('waves'), nape creamy-yellow, bill yellow. Length 85–93cm, wingspan 2.3–2.4m.

Habitat Exclusively pelagic outside breeding season; loose feeding rafts may form close to shore.

Behaviour Matures at 5–6 years; average lifespan 30–40 years. Excretes excess salt through tubes on bill. Does not follow ships, unlike many albatross species.

Breeding 1 egg laid in bare depression is incubated for 60 days. Eggs often moved up to 50m from site of laying; many get abandoned, break or are lost in crevices. Chick fledges at 167 days.

Feeding Takes large fish and squid near the surface, possibly at night; also occasionally robs boobies of food.

Voice Silent at sea; a long, loud 'mooing' during courtship displays.

Spanish *Albatros*.

Hotspots
Española (Punta Suárez) and at sea throughout Galápagos waters

A *Galápagos (wedge-rumped)* **storm-petrel** *foraging near Punta Suárez, Española.*

Audubon's shearwater *is probably the most commonly seen seabird in Galápagos waters.*

SEABIRDS

Oceanic Wanderers

Many bird families exploit the oceans' abundant food resources, but the order that includes albatrosses (p105), shearwaters, petrels and storm-petrels is adapted to a life lived almost entirely at sea. Sometimes known as 'tubenoses' because they eliminate excess salt through tubes on their bill, seabirds may spend months, or even years, traversing the world's oceans, returning to land only to nest. Storm-petrels are swallow-sized birds that patter over the water's surface as they feed, creating tiny currents which draw food towards them. Only two of the archipelago's three breeding species are common: Elliot's (white-vented) storm-petrel, which often follows boats and flies close to shore, and the Galápagos (wedge-rumped) storm-petrel, which greatly outnumbers Elliot's storm-petrels but appears less common because it's nocturnal. Larger seabirds include Audubon's shearwater, a fast-flying species that breeds in cavities in sea cliffs; feeding flocks can include hundreds of individuals. In contrast, the endangered dark-rumped petrel is usually seen wheeling over the waves alone or in small groups. Dark-rumped petrels breed only in the highlands of Floreana, Santa Cruz and San Cristóbal, where they nest in burrows and are vulnerable to predation by dogs, cats and rats. ∎

Hotspots
Genovesa Galápagos storm-petrels by the hundred thousand. **Santa Cruz** (Media Luna) Dark-rumped petrels breed in the miconia zone.

Recognition Sooty brown (almost black), pale grey crown and forehead, white 'eyelids'. Length 45cm.
Habitat Rocky coasts, pelagic.
Behaviour Sedentary; forms loose colonies. Sometimes nests in sea caves.
Breeding Downy chick fledges at 56 days.
Feeding Small fish.
Voice Usually silent.
Spanish *Gaviotín cabeza blanca.*

Hotspots
Santa Cruz (Puerto Ayora), **Isabela** (Tagus Cove)

COMMON NODDY

A Versatile Tern

Noddies are small, all-dark terns, so-called because their courtship and greeting displays involve pairs nodding their heads at each other. The common, or brown, noddy is the most frequently seen tern and the only noddy recorded in the Galápagos, where it is widespread and numbers a few thousand pairs (the sooty tern is vastly more abundant, but nests only on two northern islands, Darwin and Wolf, and is rarely seen by visitors). Noddies and terns are closely related to gulls, but have a more buoyant, graceful flight and pointed bills; common noddies are easily distinguished by their all-dark colouration and wedge-shaped tail. With so many seabirds in the archipelago, nesting sites are at a premium and the noddies seem to have drawn the short straw: their eggs and chicks are most commonly seen resting on bare, precarious ledges just above the splash zone. In the Galápagos common noddies nest year-round, although most eggs are laid between November and July and a pair may not nest every year. Common noddies feed at sea by picking small fry off the surface; they are often seen in flocks or feeding among other seabirds and may even perch on a pelican's head as it surfaces from a dive, waiting to snatch up morsels. Unlike many terns, noddies don't normally feed by plunge-diving. ∎

LAVA GULL

The World's Rarest Gull

It is estimated that only 400 pairs of lava gull exist, all of them in the Galápagos Islands, but if the current low-impact tourism and settlement policies continue the gull's future should be secure and it is not regarded as endangered. In fact, apart from its unusual and rather striking appearance – it blends in beautifully with the lava on which it often loafs – the world's rarest gull is rather typical of this cosmopolitan family. Lava gulls feed on dead fish at the tideline and eat abandoned eggs or rob them from seabird colonies; they have been recorded pirating prey from lava herons, and at sea lion colonies eat fish scraps and the placentas of newborn pups. These natural scavengers have also adapted well to the human settlement of the Galápagos, and are often seen perched around harbours or waiting near fishing boats for offal flung overboard (although unlike the flocks of scavenging gulls in some parts of the world it is rare to see more than two lava gulls together). However, breeding adults are very wary, leaving the nest when human intruders are as much as 1km away. The first lava gull nest – merely a scrape in the bare earth with well-camouflaged eggs – was not discovered until 1960 and very few have been found since. ■

Recognition Sooty-grey; white 'eyelids', red eyering, blackish bill lined scarlet.
Length 51–55cm.
Habitat Beaches, harbours.
Behaviour Nests year-round solitarily in large territories.
Breeding Chicks fledge after 60 days.
Feeding Mainly scavenges; also takes live crabs and lizards.
Voice Typical gull call.
Spanish *Gavioto de lava.*

Hotspots
Santa Cruz (Puerto Ayora), **South Plaza**, **Genovesa**

SWALLOW-TAILED GULL

Gull of the Night

Apart from a small colony in Colombia, the striking swallow-tailed gull is endemic to the Galápagos and some 10,000 to 15,000 pairs nest in more than 50 colonies scattered around all the major islands. Often touted as the world's only nocturnal gull, it feeds mainly, but not exclusively, at night and is certainly the most nocturnal of the world's 51 gull species. Its biology is not yet fully understood, but nocturnal adaptations include retinas with more rods than cones, enabling them to see contrast rather than colour, and clicking vocalisations, thought to be a basic form of echolocation that helps them to avoid obstacles in the dark.

During courtship the male presents the female with food gifts and selects a nest site; nests can be solitary or in loose colonies, but are no more than a simple scrape on the ground lined with pebbles, coral, feathers or bones. Breeding occurs year-round and colonies may have young at different stages of development; uniquely among gulls, the downy young are white, which may help parents locate them at night. At dusk swallow-tailed gulls fly out to sea to feed. They have a reputation for being rather shy at sea, but late at night you can often see their ghostly forms accompanying your boat in the darkness and hear their peculiar calls. ■

Recognition Dark-grey head, forked tail, red eyering, pied bill, pinkish legs and feet.
Length 51–58cm.
Habitat Coastal, pelagic.
Behaviour Feeds up to 500km from land; possibly locates phosphorescent prey at night.
Breeding 1 chick fledges at 58–65 days.
Feeding Squid, fish.
Voice 'Clicking' echolocation.
Spanish *Gaviota de cola bifurcata.*

Hotspots
South Plaza, **North Seymour**, **Genovesa**

Recognition Brown overall with darker scalloping, white cheeks, black-and-red bill, red eyes. Length 45cm.
Habitat Freshwater and brackish lagoons.
Behaviour Sedentary; usually seen in pairs or small flocks.
Breeding Up to 10 eggs.
Feeding Aquatic vegetation, invertebrates.
Voice Males whistle, females quack weakly.
Spanish *Patillo*.

Hotspots
San Cristóbal (El Junco Lagoon), **Santa Cruz** (Puerto Ayora), **Genovesa**

GALÁPAGOS PINTAIL

Adaptable Opportunist

A dearth of freshwater lagoons means that ducks are not common in the Galápagos, and only the Galápagos pintail breeds here (although three other species have been recorded as vagrants). The Galápagos pintail is a subspecies of the widespread white-cheeked or Bahamas pintail, and differs from its mainland relations in having less contrast between its white cheeks and the rest of its head. But it is still a handsome duck, often seen loafing tamely on the muddy shore of even the smallest pool. Like all ducks, pintails rely largely on water in which to feed and as protection for their young; the opportunistic pintail has adapted well to the challenge of living in the Galápagos, feeding both in coastal lagoons and freshwater highland pools, moving among temporary pools after rains and breeding whenever conditions permit. Galápagos pintails are so-called dabbling ducks that typically feed by upending from the surface and picking aquatic vegetation from shallow water, although they may dive in deeper water. The nest is well-hidden and built near the ground in waterside vegetation or between mangrove roots. Incubation is by the female and the young can swim and feed themselves almost as soon as they hatch, although they rely on mother's protection until fledging. Galápagos pintails number a few thousand pairs and are not endangered. ∎

Recognition Lava-coloured, grey legs (orange in breeding season), dark grey bill. Length 35cm.
Habitat Rocky shores, lagoons.
Behaviour A solitary hunter.
Breeding Normal brood 2–3 chicks; breeds throughout year when conditions suitable.
Feeding Crabs, small fish.
Voice Sharp *kyeow*.
Spanish *Garza de lava*.

Hotspots
Santa Cruz (Puerto Ayora), **Española** (Punta Suárez), **Genovesa**

LAVA HERON

The Crab-Stalking Heron

This small, endemic heron is common at the shoreline of every island and in Puerto Ayora can be seen hunting by the light of streetlights near the harbour. But during the day lava herons blend in perfectly among lava rocks and stand stock-still when hunting, and you could easily walk past several before noticing one. This diminutive species typically hunts by crouching with neck coiled, ready to strike with lightning speed. The ubiquitous sally lightfoot crab in particular is a common prey item, but lava herons are known to forage away from the shore, where they take small lizards and large insects, such as locusts. Lava herons are solitary nesters, laying their eggs on a platform of sticks on a mangrove branch or in a lava crevice, and can raise two or three broods in a good year.

The lava heron is sometimes regarded as a subspecies of the widespread striated heron; indeed, immatures of the two are virtually identical and the striated heron is clearly its immediate ancestor. However, adults look completely different and the two species coexist on many islands without interbreeding. In any case, it looks like the striated heron has invaded the Galápagos twice, once when it evolved into the lava heron, and again possibly only a few millennia ago, since it occurs on only a few islands. ∎

HERONS & EGRETS

A Deadly Grace

Even casual bird-watchers will recognise the cosmopolitan herons and egrets. Known collectively as ardeids after their family name, Ardeidae, they share features such as long legs and necks, and daggerlike bills for seizing or spearing animal prey. Only the lava heron (see opposite) is endemic to the Galápagos, but six other species are resident, ranging in size from the 30cm-tall striated heron to the 1m-tall great blue heron, and three others have been recorded as vagrants. Size disparity allows these otherwise similar birds to hunt and breed virtually side-by-side, for each species occupies a unique ecological niche and requires a different type of prey. The great blue heron, for example, typically hunts in coastal lagoons for vertebrates such as fish, rodents and young marine iguanas. The yellow-crowned night heron is a nocturnal hunter that shelters under lava overhangs during the day, emerg-

ing at dusk to feed on large invertebrates, such as crustaceans, scorpions and insects, and small vertebrates. Both the great blue heron and yellow-crowned night heron are different enough from members of the same species on the mainland to be classified as distinct Galápagos subspecies,

indicating that they have been present in the islands for a long time. But the all-white great (inset) and snowy egrets look identical to their mainland relatives and in evolutionary terms were probably recent arrivals in the Galápagos.

Two other ardeids demonstrate the phenomena of speciation and island colonisation, respectively. The cosmopolitan striated heron was the ancestor of the lava heron and seems to have re-invaded the Galápagos as it occurs only on Fernandina, Isabela, Santa Cruz, San Cristóbal and Pinta. It was first recorded breeding in the Galápagos only recently, and as hybrids have occurred some researchers still regard the lava heron as a subspecies of the striated heron.

The cattle egret is native to Africa, where it snaps up insects disturbed by herds of buffalo and elephants. But during the 20th century this extraordinary bird spread naturally all over the world to feed alongside domestic cattle and eventually arrived in the Galápagos in 1964. It is now common on the four islands with cattle (Santa Cruz, San Cristóbal, Floreana and southern Isabela) and first bred here in 1986. Feral donkeys and goats apparently don't interest the egrets, but this adaptable bird hangs around resting sea lions and even tortoises in the highlands of Santa Cruz. ■

*Although it may share roosts with other egrets, the **cattle egret** typically feeds in the highlands.*

*Red eyes help to identify juvenile **yellow-crowned night herons** from juveniles of other species.*

*Two adult **yellow-crowned night herons** sitting out the daylight hours at Punta Suárez, Española.*

*The stately **great blue heron** hunts in mangrove lagoons, along rocky shores and even in busy harbours.*

Hotspots
Santa Cruz (Puerto Ayora) Great blue herons hunt in the harbour, egrets and striated herons hunt in mangroves, yellow-crowned night herons feed under streetlights at night.
South Plaza Cattle egrets look for locusts among sea lions.
Genovesa Abundant yellow-crowned night herons.

GALÁPAGOS RAIL

An Elusive Skulker

Also known as the Galápagos crake and not to be confused with the paint-billed crake, this secretive rail is found only on islands high enough to support extensive areas of moist highland vegetation. You may be lucky enough to see one crossing the road in the highlands of Santa Cruz, where it is still relatively common, but normally this is a skulker of low, dense vegetation. Galápagos rails feed on the ground, poking into leaf litter and mosses in search of small animals, such as insects and spiders, and even climb up into shrubs in search of prey. They also inhabit fallow agricultural land on Santa Cruz, where local farmers know them as 'pachay', but they are heard far more often than seen. If you clap your hands in the right habitat several rails may call in response to the noise; they tend to run from danger, but can also be ridiculously tame and if you see one it may approach you closely. Galápagos rails are weak flyers and vulnerable to predation by dogs and cats, and rats take a toll on eggs, chicks and adults. Apart from Santa Cruz the Galápagos rail also occurs on Pinta, Fernandina, Isabela and Santiago, but is rare on San Cristóbal and there have been no records on Floreana since 1983. ■

Recognition Chocolate-brown upperparts, spotted white; grey-brown underparts; eyes red. Length 15cm.
Habitat Dense grassland, forest.
Behaviour Sedentary, monogamous, territorial.
Breeding 3–6 eggs laid September to April in ground nest.
Feeding Small invertebrates.
Voice Cackles, clucks.
Spanish *Polluela de Galápagos, pachay.*

Hotspots
Santa Cruz (Media Luna, Giant Tortoise Reserve)

AMERICAN OYSTERCATCHER

Scourge of the Tideline

Oystercatchers are striking black-and-white birds, usually seen in pairs foraging among rocks or flying down beaches uttering their piping calls. As their name suggests, they prey on bivalve molluscs, such as oysters and mussels, which they prise open with their powerful, laterally flattened bill. But oystercatchers also take other molluscs, such as snails and limpets, and employ a range of techniques, such as hammering, stabbing and probing, to get past their victims' defences. American oystercatchers are widely distributed around the Caribbean and South American coasts, but the Galápagos population shows several differences from mainland oystercatchers and could be a separate species. For example, they have shorter, heavier legs and feet, and the downy chicks have different colouration to mainland birds; and after millennia of isolation both populations may not be able to interbreed. Oystercatchers are widespread but uncommon along the coast of every island, their distribution most likely limited by the availability of feeding areas, and probably number only about 100 to 200 pairs in the Galápagos. Breeding occurs mainly from October to March; the nest is a simple scrape in the sand, and the young hatch covered in down and able to walk almost immediately. Following their parents until they fledge five weeks later, they rely on their superb camouflage when danger threatens. ■

Recognition Black-and-white. Scarlet bill, yellow eyes with scarlet eyering, pinkish legs. Length 42cm.
Habitat Rocky and sandy shores.
Behaviour Sedentary; usually seen in pairs or with recently fledged young.
Breeding 2 eggs incubated for 28 days.
Feeding Molluscs, crabs.
Voice Shrill piping.
Spanish *Ostrero.*

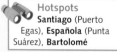
Hotspots
Santiago (Puerto Egas), **Española** (Punta Suárez), **Bartolomé**

GREATER FLAMINGO

Pretty in Pink

Flamingos are unmistakable and one of the most eagerly sought of all Galápagos birds. Their striking pink colouration is caused by carotenoid pigments ingested while feeding, either directly from algae or from plankton that have already ingested algae. But their feeding method is hardly less remarkable: lowering their elegant neck, flamingos hold their head upside-down underwater and swing that crooked bill from side to side as they walk. Using the tongue as a piston, they force water through thin plates called lamellae, which filter out living matter that is then swallowed with the aid of backward-facing spines on the tongue and palate. These ancient birds can even upend like a duck to feed in deep water. The crooked bill has evolved to maintain a constant gap when open and the bird is feeding.

Galápagos flamingos are a subspecies of the greater flamingo, which is also found in the Caribbean, but it is remarkable that they occur here at all. The greater flamingo is the largest of the world's five species, and normally requires large expanses of shallow water where colonies perform synchronised courtship dances and nest en masse. Such conditions have probably never existed in these islands and Galápagos flamingos are spread in small groups among the comparatively few available coastal lagoons. This and several other features have led some researchers to classify it as a separate subspecies. But the flamingos are not terribly abundant and although they breed here their total population is probably no more than about 500 birds. Nests are made of mud piled up in a broad cone to a height of 25cm and are vulnerable to disturbance by Galápagos sea lions at some sites; during El Niño years nests may be inundated and a whole season's breeding effort wasted. In other parts of their range greater flamingos nest well away from land-based predators in lagoons, but in the Galápagos their eggs and chicks are vulnerable to feral pigs and several erstwhile nesting colonies have been abandoned. Galápagos flamingos move around the islands and predicting their occurrence is never easy, although there are usually some at a few reliable sites. ∎

Recognition Unmistakable. Pink overall, darker on wings and legs; bill tipped black; black flight feathers visible in flight. Flies with neck outstretched. Juveniles whitish. About 1m tall.

Habitat Shallow brackish lagoons; occasionally at sea and in temporary freshwater pools.

Behaviour Sedentary; breeds in colonies of 3–50 pairs. Can feed in water to belly depth and swim in deeper water; sometimes flies between islands. Deserts nest if disturbed. Stirs up mud to flush out organisms while feeding.

Breeding Nests July to March; single young joins crèche after a week; fledges at about 70 days.

Feeding Holds head upside down while swishing bill through shallow water, filtering out algae and small animals.

Voice A gooselike *ah-ah-ah*.

Spanish *Flamenco*.

> **Hotspots**
> **Floreana** (Punta Cormorant), **Rábida**, **Isabela** (Puerto Villamil)

*A **red-necked phalarope** in non-breeding plumage; females have brighter plumage than males.*

*Lagoons near Puertos Ayora and Villamil are good spots to see the unmistakable **black-necked stilt**.*

*The **least sandpiper** is probably the most common small wader that occurs in the Galápagos.*

*Even in winter plumage, the wedge-shaped bill and orange legs identify the **ruddy turnstone**.*

SHOREBIRDS

Intercontinental Migrants

'Wader' and 'shorebird' are interchangeable terms for members of several closely related families that typically feed between the tides on a variety of small animals. Some members of two families, the plovers and the huge assemblage comprising sandpipers, godwits and stints, among others, make vast migratory journeys between their breeding grounds in the Arctic Circle and wintering areas in South America. The Galápagos Islands are ideally placed as a stopover for some of these long-distance travellers; several species of wader are commonly seen on rock platforms, beaches and shallow lagoons on most islands, and more than a dozen other species have turned up as vagrants. Many migratory waders breed among the Arctic tundra and frequent the coast only on migration; huge flocks can congregate on mainland mud flats and this is where their specialised bills come into play. Some are long and straight, some down-curved, and others short and sharp, but each is adapted for a unique feeding strategy, thus enabling many species to feed side by side.

One of the most common, and largest, migrants in the Galápagos is the whimbrel (inset), recognisable by its long, down-curved bill. Whimbrels are equally at home on the shoreline or in the highlands, where they probe for invertebrates deep in soft soil or mud. The smallest common visitor is the least sandpiper, a generalist feeder of rocky shorelines, and between the two size extremes are 'seek and peck' feeders such as sanderlings, and

grey (black-bellied) and semipalmated plovers. Sanderlings race along beaches and snatch small prey from the edge of incoming waves; the two plovers also feed along the tideline but may also frequent lagoon shores. The ruddy turnstone uses its awl-like bill to pry under rocks in search of invertebrates along rocky coasts.

Phalaropes are unusual migratory waders with lobed feet that spin on the water's surface to stir up the plankton on which they feed. In the nonbreeding season they gather at sea in great flocks, sometimes numbering thousands. One species, the red-necked phalarope, is commonly seen from boats between December and March. Most of the migratory wader species occur in the Galápagos in their rather drab nonbreeding plumage and can be difficult to identify, but two breeding residents, the American oystercatcher (p110) and black-necked stilt, are unmistakable in their black-and-white livery, the stilt also sporting ridiculously long pink legs. ∎

> **Hotspots**
> **Santa Cruz** Black-necked stilts, sanderlings, semipalmated plovers and occasional rarities at Playa Tortuga; whimbrels in the highlands at Giant Tortoise Reserve. **Santiago** (Puerto Egas) Least sandpipers, whimbrels and semipalmated plovers on rock platforms. **Isabela** (Puerto Villamil) Good wader-watching in lagoons west of town.

GALÁPAGOS DOVE

An Unusual Association

Buccaneers, who were among the first to visit the Galápagos Islands, reported how small doves clustered around them and perched on their heads. But food, not bird-watching, was high on the pirates' list of priorities; the doves were easy meat and hundreds were killed over the years. Fortunately, Galápagos doves remain common, especially where feral cats are few or absent, and relatively tame – except perhaps around human habitation. They are easily seen in arid areas of the main islands and even on beaches near landings.

The archipelago's only native dove, this bird, like so many other Galápagos birds, is a generalist feeder. It has a long bill (for a dove) that can flip over ground litter in search of seeds, of which it eats a wide variety, or snap up caterpillars and probe cactus blossoms when these become more abundant during the rains. A remarkable association has evolved on Genovesa between the doves and opuntias. There are no land iguanas to eat the cactus pads on the island, and no carpenter bees to pollinate the opuntia flowers. As a result, the cactus' stout protective spines have evolved into soft, hairlike spines through which the doves can easily pass to feed on the flowers, pollinating the cacti as they move from blossom to blossom. ■

Recognition Red-brown, iridescent neck patch and scalloped back, blue eyering, red legs. Length 18–23cm.
Habitat Arid zone.
Behaviour Nests in rock cavities year-round, sometimes twice in 1 season.
Breeding Chicks fledge at 13–17 days.
Feeding Mainly seeds.
Voice Deep *coo*.
Spanish *Paloma de Galápagos.*

Hotspots
Española (Punta Suárez), **Genovesa**, **Santa Fé**

CUCKOOS

A Controversial Invader

Only two species of cuckoo breed in the Galápagos, and the dark-billed cuckoo is reasonably common on all the larger islands except Española. These shy birds are more often heard than seen, but their chuckling *cu-cu-cu-cu-kulp-kulp-kulp* call is easy to recognise, and because it sounds like pouring water locals call the bird *'aquatero'*. It usually ducks into foliage when observed, or flies away with rapid wing beats. Dark-billed cuckoos are insect-eaters that breed with the first rains and, unlike parasitic members of this cosmopolitan family, care for their own eggs and young.

In contrast, smooth-billed anis are gregarious birds, and are often seen in rank grasslands. Although they are abundant on some islands, they were not recorded in the Galápagos until about 1960 and were probably introduced by farmers because they eat ticks off farm animals; anis are weak flyers and are unlikely to have made the long sea-crossing unaided. However, anis also rob the nests of small birds, taking eggs and chicks, and even small adults; CDRS scientists regard them as a pest because they pose a threat to endemic birds. Smooth-billed anis have been eradicated on some islands, but are still common in farmland and highlands on Santa Cruz, and on Isabela, Floreana and Santiago. ■

Hotspots
Santa Cruz Smooth-billed anis common and dark-billed cuckoos present but skulking at the CDRS. Dark-billed cuckoos among scalesia forest at Los Gemelos.

A **smooth-billed ani** at the Giant Tortoise Reserve in the Santa Cruz highlands.

Recognition Mottled dark brown, paler underparts with streaks and bars; black facial disc; piercing yellow eyes. Length 42cm.
Habitat Lava cliffs, forests.
Behaviour Nests on ground in dense vegetation, among boulders or in crevices.
Breeding Eggs laid mainly November through May.
Feeding Birds, rodents.
Voice Barking *chef-chef-chef.*
Spanish *Lechuza de campo.*

Hotspots
Genovesa, Santa Cruz (Media Luna)

SHORT-EARED OWL

The Night & Day Shift

The most common owl in the Galápagos is the same widespread species found in Europe and North America, although the very dark Galápagos subspecies should probably be regarded as a separate species. After the Galápagos hawk, this is the largest predator native to the islands and, like the hawk, it ranges widely through different habitats. Owls are typically nocturnal hunters, but on islands where the Galápagos hawk is absent short-eared owls hunt by day. The short-eared owls 'ears' are actually feather tufts at the top of the head that play no part in hearing; all owls have acute hearing which they use to locate prey on even the darkest nights. In addition, the short-eared owl's facial disc acts like a radar dish that funnels sound into its real ears, which are on the side of the head and covered by feathers. Genovesa is a particularly good place to see these birds, although they are well-camouflaged among the broken lava. On Genovesa they hunt in broad daylight among the thousands of storm-petrels or booby colonies, trying to snatch an unguarded chick. On other islands this bird is more active at dawn and dusk, and feeds principally on rodents. Short-eared owls are strongly territorial and typically hunt by quartering an area with slow, deep wingbeats, rather like a harrier. ■

Recognition Mottled golden-brown with white spots, paler underparts with black spots; black facial disc. Length 26cm.
Habitat Most habitats.
Behaviour Sometimes hunts at dawn and dusk.
Breeding 3 eggs incubated for 30 days.
Feeding Mainly rodents.
Voice High-pitched hiss.
Spanish *Lechuza blanca.*

Hotspots
Santa Cruz (Los Tuneles)

BARN OWL

Creature of the Night

The barn owl is probably as numerous as the short-eared owl in the Galápagos, but is generally more nocturnal and much less frequently seen. Barn owls are truly cosmopolitan and owe their common name to their penchant for roosting in buildings, particularly on farms, where they play a valuable role in rodent control. But they arrived in the Galápagos long before humans and are sufficiently different from their mainland relatives to be regarded as a distinct subspecies. Rodents form a significant part of the barn owl's diet in the Galápagos and the introduction of the house mouse may even have benefited it, although it also takes small birds and large insects. Barn owls occur on all major islands, but your best chance of seeing one is on islands such as Santa Cruz, where you can get out after dark. By tootling along the road you may be lucky enough to spot one sitting on a fencepost, its underwings glowing a ghostly white in the headlights as it takes off. Galápagos barn owls breed throughout the year in the lowlands, although highland birds appear to have a distinct breeding season, between November and May. Eggs are laid in a cavity on or close to the ground, especially a volcanic fissure or a hole in a tree or building; chicks fledge between 70 and 84 days. ■

GALÁPAGOS HAWK

Unusual Mating Habits

It is speculative but possible that ancestral hawks, finding an abundant food supply while using the Galápagos as a stepping stone on migration between the Americas, evolved into a distinct, sedentary species. Those birds became what we know as the Galápagos hawk and surprisingly only one species became established as a resident, although migrating ospreys and peregrine falcons still occasionally pass through. Broad-winged and as powerful as a small eagle, the Galápagos hawk is a generalist hunter that takes prey as small as insects and as large as small goats. It not surprisingly sees domestic poultry as fair game and, knowing no fear of humans, was persecuted by early settlers. Once common throughout the islands (although it apparently never lived on Genovesa, Wolf or Darwin), it is now extinct on Floreana and possibly San Cristóbal, and has dwindled to just a few pairs on Santa Cruz. The Galápagos hawk remains common only on Santa Fé and a total of about 250 birds is thought to remain in the wild throughout the archipelago. Galápagos hawks were once famously tame and have been known to perch on hats; these days they are perhaps a bit warier of people, although will still approach closely and pose for photos.

Galápagos hawks practise what is known as cooperative polyandrous breeding, whereby a female mates with several males (typically one to three, but up to seven on larger islands) who help her incubate and raise her chicks, and defend their territory. This breeding strategy is rare in birds, and usually occurs where there is a lack of breeding territories; it is not universal even among Galápagos hawks. Groups remain in their territories and group males evidently live longer than monogamous males. The stick nest always occupies a prominent position, such as a boulder with panoramic views; nests are used repeatedly and can be up to 3m deep, lined with grass, leaves and bark. The young are expelled from the nest three or four months after fledging, and spend two or three years away from territorial breeding areas before reaching sexual maturity at about three years. ■

Recognition Sooty brown with grey tail narrowly banded black; iris brown, legs and cere yellow. Immature heavily mottled overall with buffy white tail. Females larger. Length 55cm; wingspan 120cm.

Habitat Shoreline to mountain peaks, from bare lava flows to closed forest; breeds in arid zone.

Behaviour Sedentary; generally unsociable, but up to 20 birds may congregate at carcasses outside breeding season. Usually hunts from the air, gliding and sometimes hovering at 50–200m.

Breeding Varies and may be linked to weather; 1–3 eggs incubated for 37–38 days; chicks fledge after 50–60 days.

Feeding Mainly rodents, adult and young birds, such as finches, doves, mockingbirds and seabirds (especially red-footed boobies). Also locusts, centipedes, lava lizards, and hatchling tortoises and turtles. Females take iguanas, young goats and poultry; also carrion, dead fish.

Voice A far-carrying *kee-kee-kee*.

Spanish *Gavilán* or *busardo de las Galápagos*.

Hotspots
Española (Punta Suárez, Bahía Gardner), **Santa Fé**, **Fernandina** (Punta Espinosa)

*The male **vermilion flycatcher** is an unmistakable bird that occurs mainly in the highlands.*

***Barn swallows** are uncommon migrants that typically occur during the northern winter.*

*The **large-billed (Galápagos) flycatcher** is most common in the lowlands and is often rather tame.*

RESIDENT SMALL BIRDS

Filling the Gaps

Because Darwin's finches (p118) and mockingbirds fill ecological niches in the Galápagos that would be occupied by different bird families elsewhere in the world, few other passerines (perching birds) breed here. The four that do are representatives of widespread families whose ancestors were adaptable enough to exploit the archipelago's unique environment.

If any Galápagos land bird can be called ubiquitous it is the yellow warbler, which is found in every habitat from sea level to the *pampa* (high-altitude fern-sedge zone) on every island except Daphne. This is the only 'true' warbler resident in the islands and is the same subspecies that occurs on Cocos Island, off Costa Rica, showing the strong biological affiliations between the islands. These adaptable birds feed both by gleaning like a warbler and hawking like a flycatcher, and can breed several times in a good wet season.

The only other resident passerine with a claim to brilliance is the vermilion flycatcher, which is one of the New World tyrant flycatchers and a common highland bird. Males cannot be confused with any other species, although females are rather drab and look quite similar to the endemic large-billed (Galápagos) flycatcher. Both flycatchers typically feed by sallying after flying insects from a branch or post, snapping them up in midair before returning to their perch. The

large-billed flycatcher largely replaces the vermilion flycatcher in the lowlands, although there is some overlap in habitat preference and it also occurs in the highlands of Santa Cruz. Some authorities regard Galápagos vermilion flycatchers as a distinct species from mainland birds.

The Galápagos martin, resident on the southern and central islands, is sometimes regarded as a subspecies of the widespread purple martin. It is common only on Isabela and is generally most often seen in the highlands. Like other swallows and martins, it hawks for flying insects, even darting among nesting seabirds, and nests in small colonies in crevices or holes in cliffs, such as the rim of volcanic craters or sea cliffs.

Nearly every year vagrant migratory birds are recorded in the Galápagos (p137). The bobolink (inset) is seen year-round on San Cristóbal and may in fact be a resident, although no breeding has been recorded. Familiar to many North Americans, bobolinks are related to meadowlarks and typically perch on fenceposts or other vantage points in farmland. ∎

Hotspots

Santa Cruz (Los Gemelos) Vermilion flycatchers common in scalesia forest. **Fernandina** (Punta Espinosa) Yellow warblers foraging among tide pools and basking marine iguanas. **Isabela** (Volcán Alcedo) Best place to see the elusive Galápagos martin.

*Although it measures only 12cm in length, the **yellow warbler** is easily seen in all habitats.*

GALÁPAGOS MOCKINGBIRD

The Welcoming Committee

Bold, inquisitive and at times belligerent, mockingbirds are also fine songsters and always fun to watch. Individuals or family groups will often investigate tourists as they land on a beach, strutting among feet and sometimes poking into pockets and bags on the sand. There are actually four species in the Galápagos, of which the Galápagos mockingbird (right) is the most widespread and usually the first encountered as it is common around Puerto Ayora.

Galápagos mockingbirds are social birds that live in strongly territorial family parties, or gangs. Gangs forage over a wide area, generally running along the ground rather than flying, and feed cooperatively, albeit in a strict pecking order. Seeds and insects make up most of their diet, but mockingbirds are also highly opportunistic and will eat the contents of smashed seabirds' eggs and pick the ticks off land iguanas. Cooperation also extends to breeding and offspring from previous broods help their parents to raise the next clutch, feeding the youngsters and warning off intruders. Family groups stay together until the breeding season finishes.

The other three species are very similar in appearance, differing only slightly in eye colour, size and bodily proportions, but can be readily identified because they do not overlap in distribution (a trait known as allopatry). The Hood mockingbird (below) is the largest and boldest, and endemic to Española where it is easily seen. But the Chatham mockingbird, endemic to San Cristóbal, is now rare and Floreana's endemic species, the Charles mockingbird, is extinct on the main island. Its disappearance has been variously attributed to cats, rats and habitat destruction, particularly the disappearance of opuntias from Floreana, which the mockingbirds possibly favoured as a nest site. However, mockingbirds remain common on other islands with these pests and thrive in the virtual absence of opuntias on Española. The most likely answer is that Floreana never supported a native rat species, and the ecologically naive mockingbirds were unable to survive the depredations of the introduced black rat. Luckily, the Charles mockingbird survives on two small rat-free offshore islands (Champion and Gardner-by-Floreana) to which visitors are not permitted. ■

Recognition Thrush-sized with a longish, decurved bill. Streaked grey-brown upperparts with white underparts. Long tail and legs, upright stance. Eye colour variable. Length 28cm.
Habitat Sandy and rocky shores, urban gardens, arid and transition zones.
Behaviour Tame, insatiably curious and opportunistic. Dominant birds take priority at food, pecking or pushing others aside; may recognise each other by facial markings. Holds wings out for balance when sprinting. Nests in trees or prickly pears.
Breeding 3–4 eggs laid at start of the rains are incubated for 14 days; chicks fledge after 17 days.
Feeding Omnivorous; mainly seeds and insects, but also small lizards, turtle hatchlings and sea lion placentas. Around humans will try to eat almost anything.
Voice Loud, melodious whistles; also a superb mimic.
Spanish *Cucuve de Galápagos*.

Hotspots
Santa Cruz (CDRS),
Santa Fé, Genovesa

*The **warbler finch**, the smallest of the Darwin's finches, has a fine bill unlike that of any other species.*

*The **large cactus-finch** occurs on only a few islands but is generally easy to see on Española.*

*The **common cactus-finch** typically frequents opuntias, where it nests and feeds on flowers.*

DARWIN'S FINCHES

'Modified for Different Ends'

Most of the 13 species of Darwin's finch are common and easily seen at visitor sites. But they are also rather nondescript and present the biggest identification headache of all Galápagos birds. All are more or less sparrow-sized, confoundingly similar in appearance and in some plumages rather dull-looking. The bills are the key, for despite their less-than-spectacular plumage, the finches have diversified to exploit nearly every terrestrial feeding niche available to a small bird in the Galápagos. Their ancestor probably arrived long before other land birds and, finding no competition and an abundance of resources, quickly filled all niches available to it then evolved to exploit others. Just which species constituted this ancestor is still a matter of conjecture, but a likely candidate is one of the Neotropical grassquits, small enough to be blown offshore from South America but adaptable enough to survive in a new environment.

The warbler finch probably diverged first, gleaning foliage for insects and spiders with its delicate, unfinchlike bill. Indeed, few other land birds are insect specialists on the islands; in tough times seed-eaters were probably always at an advantage in this harsh environment. Adult males of six closely related species all have glossy black plumage and can only be told apart by bill shape, which varies according to dietary preference. Thus, the ground-finches – small (inset), medium, sharp-beaked and

large – between them eat seeds of every dimension, and the large and common cactus-finches exploit the blossoms of the opuntias so common in the arid zone. The three tree-finches, imaginatively dubbed small, medium and large, are arboreal specialists but also feed on the ground.

The tool use of woodpecker finches is well known, and the vegetarian finch strips bark into curls like a carpenter's plane to get at the soft tissues underneath. On Islas Wolf and Darwin, sharp-beaked ground-finches – the so-called vampire-finches – peck wounds in seabirds and drink their blood; these resourceful birds have also learned to crack seabirds' eggs against rocks and drink their contents. And other species remove parasites from iguanas and giant tortoises, the iguanas adopting a submissive posture when the birds are nearby. In the words of Darwin: '…one might really fancy that, from an original paucity of birds in this archipelago, one species had been taken and modified for different ends'. How right he was. ∎

*A female **small ground-finch** at Punta Suárez, Española. Mature males have black plumage.*

> **Hotspots**
> **Santa Cruz** Nine species; three ground-finches and the cactus-finch common around the CDRS, several others easily seen at Los Gemelos. **Española** (Punta Suárez) Large cactus- and warbler finches common along trails. **Genovesa** Your only realistic shot at sharp-beaked ground-finches.

WOODPECKER FINCH

The Finch with an Amazing Toolkit

The most famous of the Galápagos' 13 remarkable finches is undoubtedly the woodpecker finch, which makes up for its nondescript appearance by being one of the few birds in the world known to use tools. As a general principle, where there's an ecological niche to be filled something will fill it and, since the widespread woodpecker family never made it to the Galápagos (woodpeckers fly poorly across open water), one of these adaptable finches has evolved to take its place. All the Galápagos finches have bills to suit a specific feeding niche; the woodpecker finch has a stout, pointed bill and normally feeds by taking large insects from behind bark or by probing soft, decaying wood to extract soft-bodied termites and beetle larvae. Like a typical woodpecker, it forages by hopping or spiralling up trunks and branches, probing the moss and pads of epiphytes as it goes. Woodpeckers have a long, retractable tongue which the finch lacks, but some individual woodpecker finches deliberately fashion a tool to perform the same function as the woodpecker's tongue: extracting insects from their burrows. Woodpecker finches in the arid zone typically use opuntia spines, but in humid forests where there are no cacti they break off a suitable twig or leaf stem (see top right) from a tree or bush, dropping any that are unsuitable for the job because they are too short or pliable. Holding it lengthwise in its beak for maximum penetration, the bird repeatedly probes a likely looking crevice. When an insect is eventually forced out of its retreat the bird instantly drops the tool and snaps up its reward. Some individuals will carry a tool in their beak as they fly between feeding sites, trying it repeatedly until successful. Others stand on the tool or place it somewhere secure while enlarging a hole with their beak before attacking the prey again. Many species of Darwin's finches look very similar, but the woodpecker finch behaves unlike no other except the closely related mangrove finch, which also sometimes uses tools. You almost certainly won't see the endangered mangrove finch (unless you take a specialist birding tour; see p131), but the woodpecker finch is quite common in the right habitat. ∎

Recognition Large and rather drab. Uniform unstreaked olive or brown upperparts; pale yellowish or whitish underparts. Stout, pale bill turns black in breeding season. Sexes similar in appearance. Length 15cm.
Habitat Moist highlands, especially in scalesia forest and the miconia zone; also transitional and arid zones.
Behaviour Looks and probes under bark, leaves and rocks for food. Most common in highlands. May skewer prey with tool; tools may be up to 5cm in length.
Breeding Nests whenever conditions suitable in highlands or lowlands.
Feeding Omnivorous; mainly insects, which it may extract from crevices or holes in bark with a tool, but also some fruit.
Voice Loud, rapid series of 7–8 notes followed by a long *see*.
Spanish *Pinzón artesano*.

Hotspots
Santa Cruz (Los Gemelos, Media Luna, Giant Tortoise Reserve)

GREEN SEA TURTLE

Recognition Upper shell varies from blackish to olive-brown or even yellowish; head rounded and 'bill' barely hooked. Females larger. Up to 1m in length and 150kg in weight.

Habitat Inshore and offshore marine waters, sheltered lagoons; nests on sandy beaches.

Behaviour Sexual maturity reached at 20–25 years. During mating, 2 or 3 males may clamp onto the back of a female. Females delay implantation and lay 2–3 years later; may lay only once in a lifetime.

Breeding Up to 80 leathery eggs of ping-pong ball size; incubation lasts 45–55 days.

Feeding Adults mainly vegetarian, young also eat small marine animals.

Voice Silent.

Spanish *Tortuga negra*.

Hotspots
Santa Cruz (Caleta Tortuga Negra), **Fernandina** (Punta Espinosa), **Santiago** (Playa Espumilla)

The Trials of Life

Also known as the Pacific or black sea turtle, the green sea turtle is abundant in Galápagos waters and easily seen at many visitor sites. Three other species of sea turtle (hawksbill, olive ridley and leatherback) have also been recorded, but the green is the most common and the only one that breeds here. Sea turtles are exclusively marine – males spend their entire lives at sea and females return to shore only to lay eggs. With limbs modified as efficient paddles, movement on land is extremely difficult and egg-laying is restricted to beaches where the females can 'row' themselves over the sand to dig a nest. Gravid ('pregnant') females congregate inshore from December to March; this is a great time to see them underwater, and you'll also see their tracks on the dunes. After sundown they haul themselves up the beach and dig a pit above the high-water mark with their flippers; it's a laborious process that can take hours, and after covering the eggs with sand they return to the sea exhausted. Incubation relies entirely on the heat of the sun and parents never know or recognise their offspring.

On some islands feral pigs dig up and destroy whole nests, and a natural predator, the *Trox* beetle, also attacks the eggs. If a nest survives these predations, the sex of hatchlings is determined by temperature: warm sand produces females and males develop in sand under 30°C. Eggs in the warm centre of the nest are the earliest to hatch, but the movement of the first-born accelerates the hatching of the remainder so all are born more or less simultaneously. All the hatchlings wriggle upwards to wait below the surface for nightfall, then burst from the nest and race down to the sea en masse. Adult sea turtles are armour-plated and have few enemies, but the tiny young – their shell only a few centimetres long – must run a gauntlet of predators, such as frigatebirds, hawks, gulls and ghost crabs to reach the water. The survivors swim hell for leather out to sea and must survive many more years and a new suite of underwater predators before reaching maturity. ■

GIANT TORTOISE

Survival Against the Odds

A mature male giant tortoise in the wild is an impressive sight, but one that visitors will now see only on Santa Cruz, Isabela or San Cristóbal. There was once probably 200,000 throughout the Galápagos, where they evolved into 14 recognisable subspecies, but after centuries of exploitation and predation by feral animals perhaps only 15,000 to 17,000 survive. Seafarers transported thousands as fresh meat, storing them alive on their backs in ships' holds; tortoises can survive for months like this, even floating at sea, and that is probably how their ancestors arrived in the Galápagos. Finding an abundance of food they thrived here and, with no competition and no land predators, attained great size as the dominant herbivores. Giant tortoises are now extinct on Floreana, Santa Fé, Fernandina and Rábida, but the surviving subspecies occur in two main forms, serving as yet further examples of the soundness of Darwin's theories.

On arid islands where ground cover is sparse, such as Española and Pinzón, tortoises have evolved a 'saddleback' carapace (upper shell) with a raised front end that enables them to reach up to leaves. Saddleback tortoises compete aggressively at resources and rivals approach each other with heads held as high as possible; the taller animal wins and can also reach further for food. Being fitter for survival, it also passes on its genes to its offspring, perpetuating these traits. On moister islands, such as Santa Cruz, there's no need to reach up to browse on the abundant undergrowth and the tortoises have evolved domed carapaces that are enclosed at the front. Breeding strategies also differ between the two forms: dome-shaped females dig two to three nests a year with up to 20 eggs per nest; saddlebacks dig four to five nests with an average of six eggs per clutch, spreading the effort and risk of breeding.

Young tortoises make an easy snack for feral dogs and are killed by rats; feral pigs dig up and eat eggs; and feral goats compete with adults for browse. A captive-breeding program at the CDRS has had great successes, but it's a long road to recovery for decimated populations of these magnificent reptiles. ∎

Recognition Huge and unmistakable. Lower shell up to 1.5m long; total weight up to 270kg. Sexes similar, although males much larger, with concave plastron and longer, thicker tail.
Habitat Varies between islands from lush highlands to arid zone.
Behaviour Matures at 20–25 years; possibly lives 100 years. Usually active from midmorning to late afternoon. 'Domed' females descend to warmer arid zone to nest; eggs buried in cylindrical chamber and incubated by sun.
Breeding Leathery, tennis-ball-sized eggs laid June to December; incubation takes 160–240 days.
Feeding Vegetarian; known to eat more than 50 plant species, including opuntias in drier areas.
Voice Loud hisses when frightened; loud, rhythmic grunts during mating audible up to 100m away.
Spanish *Tortuga*.

Hotspots
Santa Cruz (Giant Tortoise Reserve), **Isabela** (Bahía Urvina), **San Cristóbal** (La Galapaguera)

GALÁPAGOS LAND IGUANA

Recognition Yellow-orange with dark-brown back, paler on lips and face; males attain reddish colouration in breeding season. Mature males can weigh 13kg and measure 1m. Santa Fé land iguanas paler with more pronounced spines.

Habitat Arid zone, especially near stands of opuntias and where soil is suitable for burrows.

Behaviour Lives singly or in small colonies. Males' breeding territories overlap with up to 7 female territories. Females advertise readiness to mate by raising body off ground and shaking head. May live up to 60 years.

Breeding Up to 20 eggs laid January to March in a chamber in damp soil.

Feeding Adults eat mainly opuntia pads, fruits and flowers; also carpetweed, purslane and some carrion. Young eat insects and arthropods.

Voice Silent; may hiss when threatened.

Spanish *Iguana terrestre.*

Slow Comeback for Prehistoric Survivor

Despite their large size and fearsome appearance, land iguanas are harmless vegetarians that thrive on the spiny opuntias that grow over much of the Galápagos. Like all reptiles, they have low energy requirements and can survive on comparatively little food for long periods; this helps to explain their persistence on these arid islands and how their ancestors were able to survive the sea-crossing from South America on floating vegetation. However, they never became established on several islands and the Galápagos land iguana (below) lives only on Fernandina, Isabela, Santa Cruz, South Plaza, Baltra and North Seymour. A slightly larger and paler species lives on Santa Fé (left).

Both male and female land iguanas are territorial: males will heavily defend a patch of succulent cacti with head-butting contests, and females defend their nests against other females who might accidentally dig up a clutch when excavating their own nests. Sheltering overnight in burrows, adults rely on the sun's warmth to raise their metabolism high enough to forage and generally aren't very active until midmorning. Even then they hardly go into overdrive, feeding on cactus pads, buds and flowers, although they occasionally stand on their hind legs to reach a succulent morsel. Small and medium ground-finches and mockingbirds have a symbiotic relationship with land iguanas, which adopt an erect posture if one of these birds lands on or near it. The birds hop about at will, inspecting the reptiles' skin and removing any ticks or parasites they find.

Charles Darwin once complained that he couldn't pitch a tent on Santiago because the soil was so undermined with iguana burrows. Santiago now has no iguanas, thanks to predation by rats and feral pigs, and habitat destruction by goats and donkeys. Land iguanas disappeared from Baltra during WWII, but some specimens relocated to North Seymour provided the stock for their reintroduction to Baltra. On islands where the population has been decimated the iguana's comeback has been slow, despite a CDRS breeding program; land iguanas do not reach sexual maturity for about 12 years, and in the wild many hatchlings fall prey to hawks, owls and feral pests. ∎

Hotspots
South Plaza,
Isabela (Bahía Urvina),
Santa Cruz (Cerro Dragón)

MARINE IGUANA

The Unique Sea-Going Lizard

Several other reptile groups have taken to the sea, but the marine iguana is the world's only truly marine lizard and lives only in the Galápagos. It occurs on every island in the archipelago and you will see many at close range, including semi-urbanised marine iguanas in Puerto Ayora. Marine iguanas rely on ambient temperature to regulate their body heat and therefore metabolism: if they get too cold they slow down and can die, and if they get too hot they will also expire. Early morning is the best time to see them on land; after sunrise they lie flat or broadside to the sun to warm up (probably aided by their dark colouration). By midmorning most have taken to the water to feed. Using their laterally compressed tail for propulsion, they tuck their legs along the sides of the body and dive to the bottom of tidal pools and rocky reefs to graze on seaweed growing on the sea floor. Males are strong swimmers and can dive to a depth of 10m, where they hook onto the bottom with their sharp claws before feeding. Youngsters and smaller individuals stay close to shore, feeding on algae exposed by the falling tide. Subspecies on several islands show rusty or greenish tinges, with the most spectacular extreme occurring on Española. Colour variation probably occurs when their staple is killed off during an El Niño event and they must eat red algae; at such times desperate iguanas may eat the algae growing on ships' hulls and even grass. Marine iguanas can stay submerged for up to an hour and conserve energy by lowering their heart rate, lessening the contact of warm blood to their cold exterior. But after feeding they must regain their optimum body temperature of about 37°C and climb again onto the warm rocks to bask, repositioning themselves relative to the breeze or sun to maintain a constant temperature. You may notice them ejecting two fine plumes of spray from their nostrils: this is not a defence mechanism, it is simply to rid their bodies of ingested sea salt to prevent dehydration. ∎

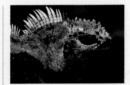

Recognition Dark grey or black, some subspecies with dull or bright red, brown or green tinges. Rounded snout and stout spines differentiate them from land iguanas. Grows to 1.5m in length and 13kg in weight.

Habitat Rocky shores and adjacent marine waters.

Behaviour Highly gregarious; huddle together to maintain warmth overnight and hundreds may align themselves similarly when sunning. Males fiercely contest territories where females bask; females defend nest burrows and may attain warning colouration.

Breeding 1–4 eggs buried in sand November to December are incubated by the sun and hatch after 3–4 months.

Feeding Dives to graze almost exclusively on marine algae, such as sea lettuce; also some animal matter, such as sea lion placenta.

Voice Silent, although agitated males may exhale loudly.

Spanish *Iguana marina*.

Hotspots
Española (Punta Suárez), **Fernandina** (Punta Espinosa), **Santa Cruz** (Puerto Ayora)

LAVA LIZARD

Recognition Slender, agile lizard with long tail; males of most species up to 20cm in length, up to 30cm on Española. Basic colouration may vary with dominant soil colour, overlaid with darker patterns; males have a spiny crest and black or yellow throat, females a red or orange throat.

Habitat Lowlands from tideline to arid and transitional zones.

Behaviour Highly active by day, hunting insects and other prey near seabird and sea lion colonies; basks on rocks, posts or even on large iguanas. Females sexually mature at 9 months and can lay clutches of eggs 3–4 weeks apart.

Breeding 3–6 eggs laid in burrows during warm season.

Feeding Omnivorous; actively hunts small invertebrates such as insects, scorpions and even smaller lizards; also flowers and other plant parts.

Voice Silent.

Spanish *Lagartija de lava.*

Animated Links in the Food Chain

Apart from large reptiles, such as the famous tortoises and iguanas, the Galápagos Islands support 10 species of gecko, a few species of harmless snake and seven species of lava lizard. Geckos hunt only at night and the snakes are uncommon, but lava lizards forage actively by day, are abundant wherever they occur and generally allow a close approach – indeed, you'll step over them as you land at several sites and sometimes see them perched on the head of marine iguanas. They chase small animals – and each other – through leaf litter, over boulders and across the sand, although being small and a prey item for many animals they dart away quickly if threatened. Lava lizards have a varied diet, but also form an important link in the terrestrial food chain and fall prey themselves to Galápagos hawks, short-eared owls, herons, mockingbirds, snakes and centipedes.

Like most reptiles, lava lizards can survive long spells without food or water and their ancestors probably drifted across to the archipelago from South America on floating vegetation. All seven species are endemic to the Galápagos and lava lizards are absent only from far-flung Genovesa, Darwin and Wolf. The Galápagos lava lizard is the most widespread species and easily seen on Fernandina, Isabela, Santiago, Santa Cruz and Santa Fé. Española, San Cristóbal, Floreana, Pinzón, Pinta and Marchena each has an endemic species, and as the Galápagos lava lizard does not occur on these islands you can be sure of any lava lizard's identification no matter which island you're on.

The various species all differ in colour and patterning, and are sexually dimorphic (ie males and females differ in size and colouration). Males (below) are larger and heavier, and have bold patterning on the back and flanks, a short crest of stout spines that can be raised during displays and a black or yellow throat. Males typically stake out a prominent boulder or post from which they 'nod' their head, their throat colouration serving as a warning to rivals or a visual cue to females. Females (inset) are smaller, rarely surpassing 18cm in length, and brighter, with a striking red or orange throat. ∎

Hotspots
Santa Cruz (CDRS), **Española** (Punta Suárez and Bahía Gardner), **San Cristóbal**

SALLY LIGHTFOOT CRAB

Colourful Patrollers of the Tideline

If any animal readily seen by visitors could be called ubiquitous, it is the large, scarlet crab that scuttles across wave-swept coastal lava from Puerto Ayora to the remotest corners of Fernandina. Dubbed sally lightfoot by English seafarers, these colourful crustaceans are not only extremely agile, as they can jump from rock to rock (try sneaking up on one for a photo), they even appear to walk on water. They really are common – not just in the red adult form, but also, if you look closely among the jumbled lava blocks, in a small dark juvenile version (top right) whose colouration blends in with the wet rocks.

Recognition Scarlet or orange legs and upper shell (often with paler ribbing), white underpart; often spotted turquoise. Juveniles almost black, becoming lighter and brighter with progressive moults. Adults up to 20cm across shell.

Although terrestrial animals, such as lizards, have tended to evolve into distinct island species throughout the Galápagos, the same species of sally lightfoot occurs on all islands. This is because its eggs hatch into the sea and the larvae drift with other plankton on ocean currents until they are large enough to settle on a rocky shore and develop into juveniles. Thus, its genetic material mixes constantly among the different island populations, whereas when a colony of lizards becomes established its gene pool is rarely, if ever, replenished with freshly drifted adults. Only a tiny percentage of larvae survive to adulthood, but the sheer number of sally lightfoots in the Galápagos indicates how many eggs must be laid each year. Called 'predator swamping', this is a common breeding strategy among invertebrates, and is thought to supply such an overabundance of food that predators can't possibly eat them all and some larvae are bound to survive.

You'll probably encounter several other crab species as you travel round the islands. Ghost crabs are quick-moving scavengers on sandy beaches that scuttle sideways into burrows when threatened. Hermit crabs have lost the ability to produce a hard shell and instead commandeer empty seashells for protection, changing to bigger shells as they grow. Fiddler crabs are most common in the sandy mud of mangroves; the males have a greatly enlarged claw which is waved about as a defence, a warning to rivals and a signal to mates. ∎

Habitat Rocky reefs and platforms, and splash zone at or above high-water mark.

Behaviour Often present in large numbers on rock platforms, scavenging large and small dead sea animals, as well as dead land animals close to the water's edge.

Breeding Each female can lay thousands of tiny eggs that hatch into planktonic larvae.

Feeding Omnivorous; adults scavenge virtually anything stranded by the tide, also preying on other crab species and even juveniles of own kind. Juveniles feed mainly on algae and detritus at or below the tideline.

Spanish *Zayapa*.

Hotspots
Santa Cruz (Puerto Ayora), **Isabela** (Tagus Cove), **Santiago**

MANTA RAY

Recognition Lozenge-shaped ray, much broader than long, with thin, whiplike tail, small dorsal fin and prominent cephalic lobes. Colour variable, from grey-blue to almost black upperparts, often with pale 'shoulder' patches; white underparts with greyish margin. Adults commonly 4–6.7m across 'wings'.
Habitat Mostly encountered over continental shelves and near offshore islands.
Behaviour Usually solitary but often in loose groups of up to 50 individuals. Spends much time near surface, occasionally leaping well clear of the water. Associates with other marine animals, such as dolphins, seabirds, sharks and eagle rays. Inquisitive and may be approached underwater. Often host to 1 or more remoras (discfish).
Breeding 1–2 live young are born in shallow water.
Feeding Filter feeds on small schooling fish and plankton, including small crustaceans, fish eggs and larvae.
Spanish *Mantarraya*.

Hotspots
Canal Bolívar Manta rays. **Santa Cruz** (Caleta Tortuga Negra) Spotted eagle rays and schools of golden rays. **Fernandina** (Punta Espinosa) Stingrays in shallow lagoons.

Winging Through the Underwater World

Although they share an ancestry with sharks, rays look like no other fish: their pectoral fins have become greatly enlarged and the body flattened, forming a diamond or lozenge shape overall. They swim by undulating their pectoral fins, giving them a graceful underwater motion not unlike flying. Of the 15 ray species recorded in the Galápagos, you'll probably see spotted eagle rays, stingrays (left) and schools of golden rays feeding in mangrove lagoons and sheltered bays. And in deeper channels you may be lucky enough to see the spectacular manta ray (below), the world's largest ray and one of the world's largest fish: some giants are reputedly 9m across the 'wings', although 4m is a more common adult size.

Despite their awesome size, manta rays are harmless filter feeders that wing through the water near the surface and scoop up mouthfuls of tiny plankton. Projecting forward on each side of the broad head are two flat 'horns' that caused superstitious seafarers to coin its alternative name, devilfish. But these fleshy extensions of the pectoral fins, known as cephalic lobes, are merely used to funnel plankton-laden water into the ray's cavernous mouth. As water enters the mouth cavity the plankton are sieved through complex filtering plates just before the gills and ingested by the ray; its rudimentary teeth appear to play no role in feeding.

Manta rays can move at a fair clip through the water and are sometimes seen making spectacular breaches. Smaller individuals may leap clear of the water by several body lengths, make several leaps in succession or even somersault. Very large specimens usually rise more or less vertically before landing on their belly or back with a loud slap, or simply sliding sideways into the sea. It is often stated that these leaps are to shake off parasites, but the rays may in fact be driving small prey animals into tightly packed balls underwater. This tactic is also employed by some whales, dolphins and sharks, and would enable a filter-feeding manta ray to gather more prey per mouthful than if it were swimming through normally dispersed schools of fish. ■

MARINE LIFE

Life Between & Below the Tides

A mixture of cool and tropical currents and diverse undersea habitats create ideal conditions for the proliferation of an amazing variety of marine life in Galápagos waters. More than 400 species of fish have been identified, of which about 10% are endemic to the archipelago. Many of the reef fish are relatively unafraid of snorkellers, and a good variety, including Mexican hogfish, yellow-tailed surgeonfish, king angelfish and concentric puffers, can easily be seen at a few choice locations. Several harmless species of shark can also be observed safely, the most common of which is the white-tipped reef shark. This small nocturnal feeder sometimes hunts inshore and is easily recognised by the white tips on its dorsal fin and tail. Fin markings also identify the black-tipped reef shark, an inhabitant of rocky reefs, which usually avoids swimmers. The most impressive species commonly encountered in deeper water is the unmistakable hammerhead, which hunts in schools and is thought to detect prey with rows of sensors along the leading edge of its distinctive head.

Marine life comes in an astonishing variety of shapes and sizes, and many thousands of species – crustaceans, molluscs ('seashells'), octopuses, squid, sea cucumbers, sea urchins and starfish (sometimes called sea stars), to name only a few groups – have been catalogued in Galápagos waters; some 800 species of mollusc alone have been identified. Particularly rich is the littoral zone (the zone below the high-water mark and as far down as light penetrates), but many creatures, especially molluscs, barnacles and crabs, eke out a living in the splash zone above the normal tidal reach.

Although the Galápagos archipelago straddles the equator, there are no coral reefs and coral grows at only a few locations. Corals are actually tiny animals related to jellyfish that live in vast colonies; the hard coral is formed of calcium carbonate secreted by these organisms to form a protective coat. Other animals likely to be encountered by snorkellers are various sea urchins, including the green sea urchin and pencil-spined urchin. The crowned sea urchin has fine black spines up to 12cm long; these nocturnal animals cluster in crevices below the low-water mark during the day. The chocolate-chip sea star is a large starfish measuring up to 15cm across that inhabits sandy seabeds. Sea cucumbers, or *pepinos* (as they are locally known), are regarded as a delicacy in some Asian cultures and have been greatly overexploited in Galápagos waters; the removal of any species from fragile marine environments can have far-reaching consequences which are as yet little understood. ■

The **chocolate-chip** (top left) and **Panamic sea stars** are two large species often seen by snorkellers.

Moorish idols can be easily recognised by their long, trailing dorsal fin and bold facial pattern.

The **Mexican hogfish**, known locally as vieja ribeteada, is common at many underwater sites.

Sheltering in crevices by day, **crowned sea urchins** emerge after dark to hunt marine invertebrates.

Hotspots
Floreana (Devil's Crown) Arguably the best snorkelling in the Galápagos, with some 50 species of fish, including Moorish idols and hammerheads. **Santiago** (Puerto Egas) Productive rock pools with starfish, molluscs and sea anemones. **Española** (Bahía Elizabeth) Sea urchins among submerged boulders, many fish and large chocolate-chip sea stars.

RESOURCE GUIDE

The following information isn't intended to be comprehensive so if you don't find it here, it doesn't mean it isn't worth checking out. But we've included some key references and contacts which we know are reliable starting points to help you find what you're looking for.

RECOMMENDED READING

Field Guides

Birds, mammals and reptiles A low species count compared to, say, mainland Ecuador, means that many recent field guides cover Galápagos birds as well as other wildlife and even plants. The only comprehensive one to vertebrates is *Birds, Mammals and Reptiles of the Galápagos Islands* by A Swash and R Still; this photographic guide is accurate and up-to-date, and is the best for identifying Darwin's finches. *Wildlife of the Galápagos* by J Fitter, D Fitter and D Hosking is another useful photographic guide, and includes many invertebrates and common plants and even covers volcanology.

Several field guides to whales and dolphins around the world are equally useful in Galápagos waters. *Whales, Dolphins and Porpoises* by M Carwardine is lightweight, covers all known species with superb illustrations and includes practical watching tips. *The Sierra Club Handbook of Whales and Dolphins* by S Leatherwood and RR Reeves is pocket-sized and comprehensive. Although it's a little bulky for a field guide, *Sea Mammals of the World: A Complete Guide to Whales, Dolphins, Seals, Sea Lions and Sea Cows* by RR Reeves et al is a superb up-to-date reference and the only guide that covers pinnipeds as well as cetaceans.

Marine life Most of the common Galápagos fish and some marine invertebrates are covered well in *Marine Life of the Galápagos: A Diver's Guide to the Fishes, Whales, Dolphins and Marine Invertebrates* by P Constant. Fish-watchers can choose from *The Fishes of the Galápagos Islands* by JS Grove and RJ Lavenberg, *Reef Fish Identification: Galápagos* by P Humann and N Deloach, and *A Field Guide to the Fishes of Galápagos* by G Merlen. Guides on invertebrates for nonspecialists include *Subtidal Galápagos: Exploring the Waters of Darwin's Islands* by J Cribb, and a series of three guides that cover most of the marine species in colour: *A Field Guide to Marine Molluscs of Galápagos* by CP Hickman and Y Finet, *A Field Guide to Crustaceans of Galápagos* by CP Hickman and TL Zimmerman, and *A Field Guide to Sea Stars and Other Echinoderms of Galápagos* by CP Hickman.

Plants Several guides are available to help you sort through the Galápagos' terrestrial plants, including *Plants of the Galápagos Islands* by EK Schofield, *Flowering Pants of the Galápagos* by CK McMullen and *Flora of the Galápagos Islands* by IL Wiggins and DM Porter. Although it's primarily a wildlife guide, *Wildlife of the Galápagos* by J Fitter, D Fitter and D Hosking includes a useful selection of commonly seen plants with colour photos.

Background Reading

Some of the following are long out of print, but should be available through a good library or online through specialist booksellers such as www.bookfinder.com or www.abebooks.com. Ornithologists and nonspecialists alike should read *The Beak of the Finch* by J Weiner, a Pulitzer Prize–winning examination of the research on Darwin's finches and its significance to the theory of evolution. Also highly readable is *The Song of the Dodo* by D Quammen for background on theories of island biogeography and the forces driving extinction. *Restoring the Tortoise Dynasty* by G Merlen is an informative, illustrated account of the fall and rise of the giant tortoises, while *Plundering Paradise: The Hand of Man on the Galápagos Islands* by M D'Orso examines the effects of tourism and other forms of exploitation in the archipelago.

Darwin's finches have been the subject of several intensive studies, starting with the seminal *Darwin's Finches* by D Lack. *Ecology and Evolution of Darwin's Finches* by PR Grant and *Evolutionary Dynamics of a Natural Population: The Large Cactus Finch of the Galápagos* by BR Grant and PR Grant are pithy but interesting tomes on this singular group of birds. *Galápagos: Islands of Birds* by B Nelson is a very readable account of a long-term study of the islands' seabirds.

Darwin in the Galápagos

Those with the time and a liking for Victorian prose should go straight to the oracle and read Charles Darwin's *On the Origin of Species*. Darwin's other musings and journals, such as *The Voyage of the Beagle: Journal of Researches into the Natural History and Geology of the Countries Visited During the Voyage of H.M.S.* Beagle *Round the World, Under the Command of Captain Fitz Roy R.N.*, are available in various formats, including edited and abridged versions. More digestible tracts include A Moorhead's *Darwin and the Beagle* (out of print but available through online booksellers) and various biographies, such as *Darwin: The Life of a Tormented Evolutionist* by A Desmond and J Moore.

Periodicals

Noticias de Galápagos is a journal published in English regularly by the Charles Darwin Foundation and includes a wide range of articles and papers about science and conservation in the Galápagos. It is available by subscription through the foundation's website (www .darwinfoundation.org).

Keep an eye on *National Geographic* and *BBC Wildlife* for articles on the Galápagos – it's never out of the news for long and constantly attracts photographers and journalists on assignment.

Bookshops

The shop at the Charles Darwin Research Station (CDRS), souvenir shops along Avenida Charles Darwin in Puerto Ayora and many tourist vessels stock several of the titles we've recommended, plus a few more general picture books. However, availability and prices are erratic and you may want to purchase them before you go. Many can be purchased online from the Charles Darwin Foundation website (www.darwinfoundation.org), and several other retailers have a web catalogue and online ordering service. As well as recent books, most of these specialised international booksellers can help

with out-of-print titles but if not, try www.bookfinder.com or www
.abebooks.com.

American Birding Association (☎ 800-634 7736, 719-578 0607;
www.americanbirding.org; PO Box 6599, Colorado Springs,
Colorado 80934-6599, USA)
Andrew Isles Natural History Books (☎ 03-9510 5750;
www.andrewisles.com; rear of 115 Greville St, Prahran, Victoria
3181, Australia)
Buteo Books (☎ 800-722 2460, 434-263 8671; www.buteo
books.com; 3130 Laurel Rd, Shipman, Virginia 22971, USA)
Charles Darwin Research Station (CDRS; ☎ 05-2526 146/147;
www.darwinfoundation.org; Puerto Ayora, Isla Santa Cruz,
Galápagos Islands, Ecuador)
NHBS Environment Bookstore (☎ 01803-865913; www.nhbs
.com; 2-3 Wills Rd, Totnes, Devon TQ9 5XN, England)
Subbuteo Natural History Books (☎ 0870-0109 700; www
.wildlifebooks.com; The Rea, Upton Magna, Shrewsbury SY4 4UR,
England)
Zoo Book Sales (☎ 507-467 8733; www.zoobooksales.com; 403
Parkway Ave N, Lanesboro, Minnesota 55949, USA)

TOUR OPERATORS

Visitor numbers in the Galápagos are strictly regulated to protect the
sensitive environment, and tour operators work to strict quotas. See
p58 for more information on travelling in the islands. Members of the
International Galápagos Tour Operators Association (☎ /fax 781-
729 6262; www.igtoa.org; PO Box 1043, Winchester, Massachusetts
01890, USA) donate a percentage of profits to projects of the GNPS
and CDRS; check out its website as a starting point when planning
your trip. Otherwise, the following operators can organise a safe,
informative and interesting wildlife-watching experience for you.

Australia
Adventure Associates (☎ 02-9389 7466; www.adventureassoci
ates.com; 197 Oxford St Mall, Bondi Junction, Sydney, NSW 2022)
South America Travel Centre (☎ 1800-655 051, 03-9642 5353;
www.satc.com.au; 104 Hardware St, Melbourne, Victoria 3000)
Tempo Holidays (☎ 03-9646 0277; www.tempoholidays.com;
1st fl, 40 Beach St, Port Melbourne, Victoria 3207)

Ecuador & Galápagos Islands
Green World Adventures (☎ 02-250 2203; www.galapagos
islands.com; Robles 653 & Amazonas Ave, 3rd fl, Office 303,
Quito, Ecuador)

North America
Ecoventura (☎ 800-633 7972, 305-262 6264; www.ecoventura
.com; 5805 Blue Lagoon Dr, Suite 160, Miami, Florida 33126, USA)
Galápagos Holidays (☎ 800-661 2512, 416-413 9090; www
.galapagosholidays.com; 14 Prince Arthur Ave, Suite 109, Toronto,
Ontario M5R 1A9, Canada)
Inti Travel & Tours (☎ 403-760 3565; www.discovergalapagos
.com; PO Box 1586, Banff, Alberta T1L 1B5, Canada)

Zegrahm & Eco Expeditions (☎ 800-628 8747, 206-285 4000; www.zeco.com; 192 Nickerson St, Suite 200, Seattle, Washington 98109, USA)

United Kingdom
Select Latin America (☎ 0207-407 1478; www.galapagos.co.uk; 79 Maltings Pl, 169 Tower Bridge Rd, London SE1 3LJ, England)
Worldwide Journeys & Expeditions (☎ 020-7386 4646; www .worldwidejourneys.co.uk; 27 Vanston Pl, London SW6 1AZ, England)

Wildlife Tour Specialists
Although any organised tour of the Galápagos is essentially a wildlife tour, some operators cater for enthusiasts with special interests, such as bird-watching or photography, and offer the best way of getting to sites not usually visited by regular tour boats. The following companies run regular tours to the Galápagos, but it's also worth checking listings of international wildlife tour operators in well-regarded wildlife magazines, such as *BBC Wildlife* and *Wildlife Conservation* (published by the Wildlife Conservation Society).

Birding Worldwide (☎ 03-9899 9303; www.birdingworldwide .com.au; Level 3, 818 Whitehorse Rd, Box Hill, Victoria 3128, Australia)
Field Guides Inc (☎ 800-728 4953, 512-263 7295; www.field guides.com; 9433 Bee Cave Rd, Bldg 1, Suite 150, Austin, Texas 78733, USA)
Naturetrek (☎ 01962-733051; www.naturetrek.co.uk; Cheriton Mill, Cheriton, Alresford, Hampshire SO24 0NG, England)
Victor Emanuel Nature Tours (☎ 800-328 8368, 512-328 5221; www.ventbird.com; 2525 Wallingwood Dr, Suite 1003, Austin, Texas 78746, USA)

PARK AUTHORITIES & CONSERVATION BODIES

A number of local and international organisations run projects and activities in the Galápagos. Contact them directly to inquire about opportunities for volunteer work or to join research and conservation expeditions.

Charles Darwin Foundation *Ecuador* (☎ 02-2244 803; www .darwinfoundation.org; Avenida 6 de Diciembre N 36-109 y Pasaje California, Quito); *USA* (☎ 703-538 6833; www.galapa gos.org; 407 N Washington St, Suite 105, Falls Church, Virginia 22046) Supports the work of the CDRS and has excellent websites covering most aspects of research and conservation in the Galápagos.
Galápagos Conservation Trust (GCT; ☎ 020-7629 5049; www .gct.org; 5 Derby St, London W1J 7AB, England) This British-registered charity raises funds for conservation in the Galápagos, and is affiliated to the Charles Darwin Foundation.
Galápagos National Park Service (GNPS; Puerto Ayora, Santa Cruz, Galápagos Islands, Ecuador)

DIVE OPERATORS

There are several dive operators in Puerto Ayora offering a range of activities for beginner, intermediate and expert divers, including certification courses. The two longest-running operators are listed here.

Galápagos Sub-Aqua (☎ 04-230 5514, 04-230 5507; www .galapagos-sub-aqua.com; Avenida Charles Darwin)
Scuba Iguana (☎ 05-526 296; www.scubaiguana.com; Avenida Charles Darwin)

WEBSITES

The following websites offer useful background information on wildlife, wildlife-watching, wildlife research and related topics in the Galápagos.

www.bbc.co.uk/education/darwin Has a good general introduction to Charles Darwin, his life and the theory of evolution.
www.camacdonald.com/birding An excellent starting point for planning a bird-watching trip to the Galápagos, with links to ecolodges, trip reports and background information.
www.enn.com The Environmental News Network is an excellent source of updates and archives on environmental issues around the world, including the Galápagos.
www.worldtwitch.com Worldtwitch is primarily a site for birders, but has useful links to Galápagos websites, news updates, books and trip reports.

GLOSSARY

For an explanation of whale- and dolphin-watching terms, see Porpoising & Other Flukish Behaviour (p39).

aa – brittle, jagged lava

adaptation – physical or behavioural trait that helps an organism survive or exploit an environmental factor

algae – *primitive* water plants, especially seaweeds

amphibian – *vertebrate* that lives part of its life cycle in water and part on land (eg frog)

aquatic – living in water or behaviour that takes place in water; compare with *marine*

arboreal – tree-dwelling

archipelago – group of islands

ardeid – any member of the heron *family* (eg heron, egret, night heron)

arthropod – *invertebrate* characterised by a segmented body and jointed legs (eg insect, spider, *crustacean*)

avian – characteristic of birds (eg avian behaviour)

avifauna – collective bird *species* of a region

beachmaster – dominant bull sea lion at a *colony*

benthic – dwelling at the bottom of the sea

biodiversity – faunal and floral richness of an area

birder – bird-watching enthusiast

bivalve – *mollusc* with shell of two hinged halves (eg mussel, oyster)

bromeliad – type of *epiphyte*

brood – group of young animals produced in one litter or *clutch*

brood parasitism – see *nest parasitism*

browse – (verb) to eat leaves and other parts of shrubs and trees; (noun) young twigs, shoots, leaves etc on which some animals feed

caldera – crater at a volcano's peak, formed when the cone collapses into the magma chamber

camouflage – colouration or patterning that helps an animal blend into its surroundings

canopy – uppermost layer of forest *foliage*, often well defined as a distinct 'roof'

carapace – upper shell, usually applied to giant tortoises, *marine* turtles and *crustaceans*; see also *plastron*

carnivore – meat-eating animal

carrion – dead or decaying flesh

CDRS – Charles Darwin Research Station

cere – fleshy, often colourful area at the base of a bird's bill

cetacean – collective term for whales, dolphins and porpoises

class – major division of animal classification (eg *mammal*, bird, reptile)

clutch – number of eggs laid at a time

colony – congregation of animals (eg birds) that live, *roost* or breed together

commensalism – relationship between two unrelated animal *species* in which one *species* benefits from the interaction and the other is unaffected

courtship – behaviour (often ritualised) associated with attracting a mate

crèche – young birds or *mammals* gathered for safety and play

crepuscular – active at dawn and dusk

crustacean – *arthropod* with gills, which can breathe underwater or survive in damp conditions on land (eg crab)

cryptic – behaviour, appearance or lifestyle that helps conceal an organism from predators

deciduous – shedding all leaves annually, usually in response to seasonal shortages in nutrients or water

decurved – downward-curving (eg in beaks or claws)

dimorphism – having two forms of colour, shape or size (eg bull and cow sea lions); see also *sexual dimorphism, polymorphism*

display – behaviour transmitting information from the sender to another, often associated with threat, defence of *territory, courtship* etc

diurnal – active during daylight hours; opposite of *nocturnal*

divergence – evolution of a different *species* from a common ancestor

dorsal – pertaining to upper (top) surface, ie the back, on most animals; opposite of *ventral*

down – loose, fluffy feathers that cover young birds and insulate *plumage* of adults

driblet cone – small cone formed by escaping gases or steam; also called *hornito* (Spanish)

echolocation – method by which *cetaceans* and bats determine their surroundings by reflected high-frequency sounds; often used to locate prey

ecology – scientific study of relationships between organisms, their environment and each other

ecosystem – community of living organisms and their physical environment

endangered – in danger of imminent extinction if trends causing its demise continue

endemic – native and restricted to a certain area (eg the flightless cormorant is endemic to the Galápagos)

epiphyte – plant that gathers nutrients and water from the air, usually growing on another plant for support (eg orchids on a tree); sometimes called air plant

equatorial – on or near the equator

estrus – see *oestrus*

family – scientific grouping of related *genera,* eg Otaridae (the sea lion family)

feral – running wild, especially escaped domestic stock or introduced *species*

fledgling – young bird able to leave the nest (ie to fledge)

flight feathers – large wing feathers; also called *primary feathers*

foliage – leafy vegetation (eg on trees)

garúa – fine mist caused by temperature inversion during the cool season (usually June to November)

genera – plural of *genus*

generalist – *species* that can tolerate a broad range of *habitats* and food

genus – taxonomic grouping of closely-related *species*

gestation – period that young *mammals* develop in the womb before birth

GNP – Galápagos National Park

GNPS – Galápagos National Park Service

gravid – pregnant (also applies to reptiles or birds carrying eggs)

gregarious – forming or moving in groups (eg herds or flocks)

guano – phosphate-rich excrement deposited by birds and bats, accumulated over generations

gular pouch – naked throat pouch, characteristic of pelicans and allies

habitat – environment in which an organism is normally found

hawk – to fly actively in search of prey, such as insects, usually caught in the open mouth

helper – animal, usually from a previous *brood,* which helps parents raise subsequent offspring (eg Galápagos mockingbird)

herbivore – plant-eating animal

hierarchy – order of dominance among social animals, usually with a dominant individual or caste and one or more tiers of status or function

home range – area over which an individual or group ranges over time; compare with *territory*

hornito – 'little oven'; also called *driblet cone* (Spanish)

host – organism on (or in) which a *parasite* lives; bird that raises young of parasitic *species*

hybrid – offspring, usually infertile, resulting from a mating between two different *species*; rare among *vertebrates*

immature – *stage* in a young bird's development between juvenile and adult

invertebrate – animal without a spinal column or backbone (eg insect, worm)

iridescence – metallic sheen on many insects and birds (eg Galápagos dove)

juvenile – animal between infancy and adulthood *(mammals)* or with first feathers after *natal down* (bird)

kleptoparasite – animal that steals food obtained by another (eg frigatebird)

lamellae – thin comblike plates in the bill of some birds (eg flamingos) that filter food particles from water

lanugo – coat of fur with which sea lions are born; later shed

lava tube – natural, often circular tunnel formed by lava flow

littoral – pertaining to the *habitat* between high and low tides; also to maximum depth where *photosynthesis* is possible underwater

loaf – to laze about, especially used in describing bird behaviour

mammal – warm-blooded, usually furry or hairy animal (except *cetaceans*) that gives birth to and suckles live young

mandible – lower part of beak or jaw in *vertebrates* or the main mouthparts in *invertebrates* (eg 'pincers' in biting ants)

marine – living in the sea; compare with *aquatic*

matrilineal – relating to kinship or descent among related females

migration – regular movement, often en masse, from one location to another usually in response to fluctuating levels of a critical resource such as food; compare with *resident*

mollusc – soft-bodied, unsegmented animal, usually with a shell (eg snail, mussel)

monogamous – having one reproductive partner for life or breeding season

mortality – (as used here) an environmental factor causing death

moult – to shed and replace all or certain feathers, skin or fur, usually prompted by seasonal or behavioural factors (eg *courtship,* onset of summer)

natal – pertaining to birth

Neotropics – tropical regions of the New World (ie most of Latin America); see *tropical*

nest parasitism – laying eggs in the nest of another bird *species* and taking no further part in rearing the offspring (eg cuckoos); also called *brood parasitism*

nestling – young bird until it leaves the nest; compare with *fledgling*

niche – role of an organism within a community (ie its preferred *habitat*), its place in the food chain, and effect on the environment and other *species*

nocturnal – active at night; opposite of *diurnal*

oestrus – period when female *mammal* is ovulating and therefore sexually receptive (also spelt estrus)

offing – expanse of sea visible from a vantage point such as a headland

omnivore – animal that eats both plant and animal matter

order – grouping of one or more related animal families; eg cats, dogs and sea lions belong to order Carnivora *(carnivores)*

pahoehoe – twisting, rope-like lava

pair bond – social ties that keep a mated pair together, reinforced with grooming, calls etc

pampa – high-altitude fern-sedge *habitat*

panga – dinghy; small boat used to ferry passengers (Spanish)

parasite – plant or animal that obtains nourishment during all or part of its life from another life form, usually to the detriment of the *host*

passerine – usually small, 'perching' birds and songbirds

of the *order* Passeriformes (eg finch, mockingbird)

pelagic – living at sea (ie in or above open water)

pepino – sea cucumber (Spanish)

phosphorescent – luminescence produced without heat by many small *marine* animals

photosynthesis – process whereby plants convert sunlight, water and carbon dioxide into organic compounds

pinniped – any member of the *mammal* families that include seals, sea lions, fur seals and walruses

pioneer – first animal or plant *species* to colonise an area; most often applied to rapidly growing plants that appear first after clearing

plankton – small *marine* plants and animals that drift on the ocean's surface

plastron – hard plate forming the lower half of a tortoise or sea turtle's shell; see also *carapace*

plumage – birds' feathers, often used to describe total appearance (eg drab plumage)

pneumatophore – aerial root enabling a mangrove to 'breathe'

pod – coordinated, social group of *cetaceans,* especially toothed whales

polyandry – female having access to more than one reproductive male

polygamy – having access to more than one reproductive mate

polygyny – male having access to more than one reproductive female

polymorphism – having more than one adult form, size or colour (eg red-footed booby)

porpoising – term used for *cetacean* or *pinniped* leaping from the water while travelling at speed

primary feathers – see *flight feathers*

primitive – resembling or representing an early *stage* in the evolution of a particular group of animals

quarter – to systematically range over an area in search of prey (eg birds of prey)

race – see *subspecies*

raptor – bird of prey (eg hawk, falcon)

regurgitate – to bring up partly digested food from crop or stomach, particularly when feeding young

resident – animal remaining in a particular area for the reproductive *stage* of its life cycle, usually associated with territorial behaviour; also, as applied to birds, remaining in a region or country for its entire life (compare with *migration*)

rodent – any of the many *species* of rat, mouse, squirrel, porcupine etc

roost – area where *mammals* (eg bats) or birds gather to sleep, sometimes in large numbers

rump – upper backside of *mammal* or bird, often distinctively marked for *signalling*

saddle – mid to lower back area on *mammals* and birds

sanguivore – blood-eating animal (eg vampire-finch)

scavenger – animal that feeds on *carrion* or scraps left by others

scrape – shallow digging in soil used by some birds, such as gulls, as a nest

selection – process by which environmental or behavioural pressures weed out traits that are detrimental to an organism's reproductive success or favour traits which aid that success

sexual dimorphism – differences in colour, size or form between males and females of the same *species* (eg bull and cow sea lions); many spectacular examples in birds

shorebirds – see *waders*

signal – behaviour or *display* that conveys information from one animal to another (eg of danger)

spawn – eggs of fish and *amphibians,* usually laid in water

speciation – process whereby *species* are formed from a common ancestor

species – organisms capable of breeding with each other to produce fertile offspring; distinct and usually recognisable from other species

spy-hopping – behaviour in *marine species* (whales and sharks) of peering above water's surface apparently to check bearings, threats etc

stage – level in development of an organism

streamer – long tail feather (eg of red-billed tropicbird)

subadult – last *stage* of juvenile development, usually characterised by near-adult colouration, size or *plumage*; distinct from adult in generally being nonreproducing

subspecies – population of a *species* isolated from other populations (eg by landforms) that has developed distinct genetic, physical or behavioural traits over many generations (also called *race*); can interbreed successfully with other subspecies of the same species but usually does not due to discrete distributions

succession – natural process whereby *ecosystems* are replaced by others over time

succulent – plant adapted to arid *habitats* with fleshy moisture-holding leaves and/or stems

taxonomy – scientific classification of organisms according to their evolutionary relationships; also called systematics

tectonic – pertaining to changes in the earth's crust caused by movement of molten rock below its surface

terrestrial – living on the ground

territory – area inhabited by an individual, defended against others of the same *species* (and usually the same sex) to provide exclusive access to resources such as food, mates, den sites etc; compare with *home range*

thermal – (noun) rising column of warm air, used by birds (especially raptors) to gain height; (verb) describing this behaviour

thermoregulation – control of body temperature, either internally or by altering behaviour

thigmotactic – seeking body contact to maintain heat (eg Galápagos sea lions)

tool-use – manipulation of a naturally-occurring object, usually as an aid to food-gathering (eg use of cactus spines by woodpecker finches)

tropical – found within the tropics (ie between tropics of Cancer and Capricorn)

tubenose – seabird with salt-regulating nasal tube (eg albatross, shearwater, storm-petrel)

understorey – layer of vegetation growing beneath the *canopy*

upwelling – stream of nutrients forced towards the ocean's surface by rising underwater currents

vagrant – migratory individual recorded outside the usual range for its *species*

vascular plants – 'higher' plants, with rigid stems and internal vessels for fluid transport (eg trees, opuntias, flowers)

ventral – pertaining to lower (under) side of an animal; opposite of *dorsal*

vertebrate – animal having a backbone (ie fish, *amphibian,* reptile, bird or *mammal*)

vocalisation – sound made orally by an animal, usually with a specific communicative meaning

waders – shorebirds and related families (eg plovers)

warm-blooded – maintaining a constant body temperature by internal regulation (eg most birds and *mammals*); more accurately known as homeothermic

waterfowl – general term for water-dwelling birds with webbed feet (eg swans, geese and ducks)

GALÁPAGOS WILDLIFE CHECKLIST

Use this list to check off what you see as you travel round the islands. Page numbers are given for the relevant references in the Wildlife Gallery (p93). Symbols indicate whether an animal is an endemic species [*], an endemic subspecies [**], introduced [i], a resident [r], a regular migrant [m], a vagrant [v] recorded only occasionally, or status unknown [?].

MAMMALS

Sea Lions
☐ Galápagos sea lion* (p97)
☐ Galápagos fur seal* (p96)

Rodents
☐ Santiago rice rat*
☐ small Fernandina rice rat*
☐ large Fernandina rice rat*
☐ Santa Fé rice rat*
☐ house mouse [i]
☐ black (ship) rat [i]
☐ brown (Norway) rat [i]

Bats
☐ hoary bat [r]
☐ Galápagos red bat**

Whales & Dolphins
☐ minke whale [m]
☐ sei whale [v]
☐ Bryde's whale [r]
☐ fin whale [v]
☐ blue whale [v]
☐ humpback whale [m]
☐ sperm whale [r]
☐ dwarf sperm whale [v]
☐ pygmy sperm whale [v]
☐ Blainville's beaked whale [v]
☐ gingko-toothed whale [v]
☐ Cuvier's beaked whale [v]
☐ killer whale (orca) [r] (p99)
☐ false killer whale [m]
☐ short-finned pilot whale [r]
☐ melon-headed whale [v]
☐ pygmy killer whale [v]
☐ common dolphin [m]
☐ striped dolphin [m]
☐ long-snouted spinner dolphin [m]
☐ pantropical spotted dolphin [m]
☐ Risso's dolphin [m]
☐ Fraser's dolphin [v]
☐ rough-toothed dolphin [v]
☐ bottlenose dolphin [r] (p98)

BIRDS

Seabirds
☐ Galápagos penguin* (p100)
☐ waved albatross* (p105)
☐ Audubon's shearwater** (p106)
☐ sooty shearwater [m]
☐ dark-rumped petrel** (p106)
☐ Galápagos (wedge-rumped) storm-petrel** (p106)
☐ Elliot's (white-vented) storm-petrel** (p106)
☐ band-rumped storm-petrel [r]
☐ brown pelican** (p102)
☐ Nazca booby [r] (p104)
☐ red-footed booby [r] (p104)
☐ blue-footed booby** (p104)
☐ flightless cormorant* (p101)
☐ great frigatebird [r] (p103)
☐ magnificent frigatebird** (p103)
☐ red-billed tropicbird [r] (p102)

Ducks & Grebes
☐ Galápagos pintail** (p108)
☐ blue-winged teal [m]
☐ masked duck [v]
☐ black-bellied whistling-duck [v]
☐ pied-billed grebe [v]

Crakes & Rails
- ☐ paint-billed crake [r]
- ☐ Galápagos rail* (p110)
- ☐ sora [v]
- ☐ common moorhen (gallinule) [r]
- ☐ American purple gallinule [v]
- ☐ American coot [v]

Flamingos
- ☐ greater flamingo** (p111)

Herons & Egrets
- ☐ great blue heron** (p109)
- ☐ tricolored heron [v]
- ☐ little blue heron [v]
- ☐ cattle egret [r] (p109)
- ☐ snowy egret [m] (p109)
- ☐ great egret [r] (p109)
- ☐ yellow-crowned night heron** (p109)
- ☐ black-crowned night heron [v]
- ☐ striated heron [r] (p109)
- ☐ lava heron* (p108)

Gulls, Terns & Skuas
- ☐ swallow-tailed gull* (p107)
- ☐ lava gull* (p107)
- ☐ Franklin's gull [m]
- ☐ laughing gull [m]
- ☐ kelp gull [v]
- ☐ common (brown) noddy** (p106)
- ☐ sooty tern [r]
- ☐ black tern [v]
- ☐ common tern [m]
- ☐ royal tern [m]
- ☐ white tern [v]
- ☐ pomarine jaeger (skua) [v]
- ☐ South Polar skua [v]

Waders or Shorebirds
- ☐ American oystercatcher** (p110)
- ☐ black-necked stilt [r] (p112)
- ☐ black turnstone [v]
- ☐ surfbird [m]
- ☐ ruddy turnstone [m] (p112)
- ☐ willet [m]
- ☐ short-billed dowitcher [m]
- ☐ Hudsonian godwit [v]
- ☐ whimbrel [m] (p112)
- ☐ marbled godwit [v]
- ☐ lesser yellowlegs [m]
- ☐ greater yellowlegs [v]
- ☐ pectoral sandpiper [v]
- ☐ buff-breasted sandpiper [v]
- ☐ stilt sandpiper [m]
- ☐ red knot [m]
- ☐ sanderling [m] (p112)
- ☐ spotted sandpiper [m]
- ☐ wandering tattler [m]
- ☐ solitary sandpiper [m]
- ☐ least sandpiper [m] (p112)
- ☐ semipalmated sandpiper [v]
- ☐ western sandpiper [v]
- ☐ white-rumped sandpiper [v]
- ☐ Baird's sandpiper [v]
- ☐ red (grey) phalarope [m]
- ☐ red-necked phalarope [m] (p112)
- ☐ Wilson's phalarope [m]
- ☐ Wilson's plover [v]
- ☐ killdeer [v]
- ☐ semipalmated plover [m] (p112)
- ☐ Pacific golden plover [v]
- ☐ American golden plover [v]
- ☐ grey (black-bellied) plover [m] (p112)

Hawks & Falcons
- ☐ Galápagos hawk* (p115)
- ☐ osprey [m]
- ☐ peregrine falcon [m]

Owls & Nightjars
- ☐ short-eared owl** (p114)
- ☐ barn owl** (p114)
- ☐ common nighthawk [v]

Kingfishers
- ☐ belted kingfisher [m]

Pigeons & Doves
☐ Galápagos dove* (p113)
☐ feral pigeon [i]
☐ eared dove [v]

Cuckoos
☐ dark-billed cuckoo [r] (p113)
☐ black-billed cuckoo [v]
☐ smooth-billed ani [i] (p113)
☐ groove-billed ani [r?]

Swallows, Swifts & Martins
☐ chimney swift [v]
☐ Galápagos martin* (p116)
☐ purple martin [m]
☐ barn swallow [m]
☐ bank swallow (sand martin) [v]
☐ cliff swallow [v]

Flycatchers
☐ vermilion flycatcher** (p116)
☐ eastern kingbird [v]
☐ large-billed (Galápagos) flycatcher* (p116)

Warblers, Tanagers & Buntings
☐ yellow warbler** (p116)
☐ blackpoll warbler [v]
☐ bananaquit [v]
☐ red-eyed vireo [v]
☐ cedar waxwing [v]
☐ summer tanager [v]
☐ rose-breasted grosbeak [v]
☐ indigo bunting [v]
☐ bobolink [m] (p116)

Mockingbirds
☐ Chatham mockingbird* (p117)
☐ Charles mockingbird* (p117)
☐ Galápagos mockingbird* (p117)
☐ Hood mockingbird* (p117)

Darwin's Finches
☐ small ground-finch* (p118)
☐ medium ground-finch* (p118)
☐ large ground-finch* (p118)
☐ sharp-beaked ground-finch* (p118)
☐ common cactus-finch* (p118)
☐ large cactus-finch* (p118)
☐ vegetarian finch* (p118)
☐ small tree-finch* (p118)
☐ medium tree-finch* (p118)
☐ large tree-finch* (p118)
☐ woodpecker finch* (p119)
☐ mangrove finch* (p118)
☐ warbler finch* (p118)

REPTILES
☐ giant tortoise* (p121)
☐ green sea turtle [m] (p120)
☐ leatherback turtle [m]
☐ olive ridley turtle [m]
☐ hawksbill turtle [m]
☐ marine iguana* (p123)
☐ Galápagos land iguana* (p122)
☐ Santa Fé land iguana*
☐ Galápagos lava lizard* (p124)
☐ Española lava lizard* (p124)
☐ Floreana lava lizard* (p124)
☐ Marchena lava lizard* (p124)
☐ Pinta lava lizard* (p124)
☐ Pinzón lava lizard* (p124)
☐ San Cristóbal lava lizard* (p124)

140

INDEX

RESEARCH

The author visited as many of the islands as possible during the research for this book. In cases where access was not possible, material was drawn from sources such as scientific papers and authoritative publications, and corroborated by experts. In his research the author has drawn on his experience, his contacts and his personal observations. He has not necessarily been able to see everything and has not gone on every available tour. Instead, he has used his expertise to judge what to bring together in as accurate a picture of a place as possible. Common names for many wide-ranging mammals and birds vary around the globe, and no two references agree completely on names (scientific or common). Mammal names used in this book follow *Sea Mammals of the World* by RR Reeves, BS Stewart, PJ Clapham and JA Powell. For birds we followed the *Handbook of the Birds of the World*, edited by J del Hoyo, A Elliott and J Sargatal.

THE LONELY PLANET STORY

The story begins with a classic travel adventure: Tony and Maureen Wheeler's 1972 journey across Europe and Asia to Australia. There was no useful information about the overland trail then, so Tony and Maureen published the first Lonely Planet guidebook to meet a growing need.

From a kitchen table, Lonely Planet has grown to become the largest independent travel publisher in the world, with offices in Melbourne (Australia), Oakland (USA) and London (UK). Today Lonely Planet guidebooks cover the globe. There is an ever-growing list of books and information in a variety of media. Some things haven't changed. The main aim is still to make it possible for adventurous travellers to get out there – to explore and better understand the world.

At Lonely Planet we believe travellers can make a positive contribution to the countries they visit – if they respect their host communities and spend their money wisely. Every year 5% of company profit is donated to charities around the world.

Lonely Planet Offices

Australia
Head Office
Locked Bag 1, Footscray
Victoria 3011
☎ 03 8379 8000
fax 03 8379 8111
talk2us@lonelyplanet.com.au

USA
150 Linden St, Oakland
CA 94607
☎ 510 893 8555
toll free 800 275 8555
fax 510 893 8572
info@lonelyplanet.com

UK
72–82 Rosebery Ave
Clerkenwell, London
EC1R 4RW
☎ 020 7841 9000
fax 020 7841 9001
go@lonelyplanet.co.uk

Send Us Your Feedback

We love to hear from travellers – your comments keep us on our toes and help make our books better. Our well-travelled team reads every word on what you loved or loathed about this book. Although we cannot reply individually to postal submissions, we always guarantee that your feedback goes straight to the appropriate authors, in time for the next edition. Each person who sends us information is thanked in the next edition – and the most useful submissions are rewarded with a free book.

To send us your updates – and find out about Lonely Planet events, newsletters and travel news – visit our award-winning website: **www.lonelyplanet.com/feedback**.

Note: We may edit, reproduce and incorporate your comments in Lonely Planet products such as guidebooks, websites and digital products, so let us know if you don't want your comments reproduced or your name acknowledged. For a copy of our privacy policy visit www.lonelyplanet.com/privacy.

Map Legend

HYDROGRAPHY

Reef
Coastline
River, Creek
Lake
Intermittent Lake
Beach
Spring/Waterhole
Waterfalls
Swamp

ROUTES & TRANSPORT

Freeway
Highway
Major Road
Minor Road
Vehicle Track
Walking Track
Fence
Ferry Route
Train Route & Station
A10 Route Number

BOUNDARIES

International
Provincial
Marine Park

MAP SYMBOLS

◌ **CAPITAL** National Capital
◎ CAPITAL Regional Capital
● CITY City
● Town Town
● Village Village
● Point of Interest
● Geographic Feature
● Hydrographic Feature
● Reserve, Wildlife Park
✈ Airport
Airfield
Boat Anchorage
Camp Site
Cave
Cliff, Escarpment
Fissures
Forest
Gate
Hotel
Lodge, Hut
Lookout, Viewpoint
▲ Mountain, Hill
Picnic Site
Ruins
Tourist Information
Volcano

AREA FEATURES

Galápagos National Park
(Primitive Zone)
Galápagos National Park
(Max. Protection Zone)
Non-GNP Area
Military Area
Lava Flow

ABBREVIATIONS

BR Botanical Reserve
CA Conservation Area
CP Conservation Park
CR Conservation Reserve
FR Forest Reserve
GR Game Reserve
MP Marine Park
MNP Marine National Park
MNR Marine National Reserve
NP National Park
NR National Reserve
NrP Nature Park
PN Parque Nacional
RR Regional Reserve
SF State Forest
SR State Reserve
WP Wetland Park
WR Wildlife Reserve

*Note: not all symbols displayed
above appear in this book*